PAUL BUNYAN
A Timeless American Legend

James Stevens was a favorite poet of many in his native Northwest. A contemporary of writers like H.L. Davis and Steward Holbrook he shared their deep love of nature and the land in which they lived — rich in forestland and timber. It was only natural that he sensed the change that was about in America in the twenties and it was also quite natural for him to gather from the logging camps and cookhouses the key stories that made up the legend of *Paul Bunyan*.

At the urging of H.L. Mencken he brought the twelve classic tales together in one volume and published them. This edition is a reprint of that classic first published in 1925 and it contains the original woodcuts by Allen Lewis. It became a national bestseller and awakened a generation to a forgotten treasure of folklore. We hope that this new edition will do the same for a new generation of readers.

PAUL BUNYAN

James Stevens

Woodcuts by
Allen Lewis

Comstock Editions

To Otheman Stevens,

Additional copies of this book may be obtained by sending a
check or money order for the price of the book plus one dollar
for the first copy and seventy-five cents for each additional
copy. A free catalog of books published by Comstock is
available by mail from this address:

COMSTOCK EDITIONS, INC.
3030 Bridgeway, Sausalito, CA 9496

CONTENTS

INTRODUCTION

THE Paul Bunyan legend had its origin in the Papineau Rebellion of 1837. This was a revolt of the
French-Canadians against their young English queen.
In the Two Mountains country, at St. Eustache, many
loggers armed with mattocks, axes, and wooden forks
which had been steamed and warped into hooks,
stormed into battle. Among them was a mighty-
muscled, bellicose, bearded giant named Paul Bunyon.
This forest warrior, with a mattock in one hand, and
a great fork in the other, powerful as Hercules, indomitable as Spartacus, bellowing like a furious
Titan, raged among the Queen's troops like Samson
among the Philistines. He came out of the rebellion
with great fame among his own kind. His slaughters
got the grandeur of legend.

Later this Paul Bunyon operated a logging camp.
In that day logging was heroic labor. In the autumn
the loggers went to the woods, forcing their way in
batteaux up swift rivers. On every trip there were
many wearisome portages around rapids. Snow and
ice then locked them in their camps for five or six
months. The workday was from dawn to dusk.
The loggers lived on beans, salt pork and sourdough
bread. At night there were songs and tales around
the shanty stove. Of course these were mainly about

their own life, their own heroes.   The camp boss was like the chief of a tribe; his will had to be the law, and he had to have exceptional physical power and courage to enforce it.   After his part in the rebellion there was no more famous camp chief in Canada than Paul Bunyon.

Sure that the Paul Bunyan stories which have been told for generations in the American timberlands were of Canadian origin, I questioned many old time French-Canadian loggers before I found genuine proofs.   At last I met Louis Letourneau in the Big Berry country, Puyallup, Washington.   And Louis' father-in-law, Z. Berneche, a snowy-maned, shining-eyed, keen-minded veteran logger of ninety years, told me about the original hero.   His uncle, Collet Bellaine, fought by the side of Paul Bunyon, and later worked two seasons for him.   Now, the French-Canadians have no genius for the humor of purposeful exaggeration such as the Americans have; the *habitans* exaggerate honestly and enthusiastically and with an illusion of truth, like Tartarin of Tarascon.

"My uncle, Collet Bellaine," said Mr. Berneche earnestly, "know that Paul Bunyon carry five hundred pounds on portage.   That is truth.   He was very big, strong man, you understand; he fight like hell, he work like hell, and he pack like hell.   Never was another man like Paul Bunyon.   That's right."

It is not difficult to imagine the *habitans* honestly exaggerating the logging feats of the war hero as they talked about him in the New Brunswick camps, and in

Maine, and in the Great Lakes pineries. And it is simple for one who has seen the two races together to imagine the Americans "improving" on the first stories about Paul Bunyon, only to ridicule his extravagant admirers; and then developing their own Paul Bunyan legend to ease their weariness when their twelve-hour day was done.

Other evidence supports this view of the origin of the stories. There are stories told about an Irish-French-Canadian logger, Joe Mufraw (Murphy was his ancestral name); and the name of Joe Mufraw is famous in the woods, sometimes being linked with Paul Bunyan's. He appears in the Red River Lumber Company's collection of Paul Bunyan stories. Now, Joe Mufraw logged in the Misstassinny River country in Quebec less than fifty years ago. I have seen pictures of this huge frowning man and his oxen. Many old French-Canadians have sworn to me that he put the calks in his boots in the shape of his initials, and that after the thirteenth drink he would kick his initials in a ceiling eight feet high. His feats in camp and on the log drives were as magnificent.

It was the American loggers below the Border who made of Paul Bunyon a true hero of camp nights' entertainment. They gave him Babe, the blue ox, who measured forty-two ax handles and a plug of chewing tobacco between the horns. They created the marvelous mythical logging camp, with its cookhouse of mountainous size and history of Olympian feats; and they peopled this camp with astound-

ing minor heroes. They made their Paul *Bunyan*
an inventor and orator, and an industrialist whose
labors surpassed those of Hercules. They devised
a chronology for him; he ruled American life in
the period between the Winter of the Blue Snow
and the Spring That the Rain Came Up From China.
By 1860 Paul Bunyan had become a genuine American
legendary hero.

Perhaps the Paul Bunyan narrator who won most
lasting fame was Len Day, whose firm of Len Day &
Son was one of the largest lumber concerns of Minne-
apolis in the sixties. I had often heard of him;
and lately Mr. Michael Christopher Quinn, yard
superintendent for the Northwestern Lumber Company, of Hoquiam, Washington, for twenty-two years,
gave me a first-hand account of him. In 1873 Mr.
Quinn was working in a great log drive down the
Mississippi; his camp was at Haney Landing, Minne-
sota. Len Day was then eighty-five, a prosperous
and influential lumberman. But the lure of the drive
and of camp life still stirred the true logger's soul of
him, and he came to the camp each spring. Every
night the gang gathered in the cookhouse to hear the
old camp bard declaim a canto of the Paul Bunyan
epic.

"Len Day told the stories in sections," said Mr.
Quinn.

A section, or a canto, or a chapter, or whatever one
may call it, was delivered each night by the old
lumberman, who could see toiling demi-gods and
sweating heroes in his dark woods, and imagined

narratives about them, to which he gave the substance
and characters of the traditional Paul Bunyan stories.
Len Day had lived in New Brunswick in the forties
and had thus heard the stories in their beginnings.
The Paul Bunyan stories which form the body of
the legend have not had many changes or surviving
additions in fifty years. They themselves are not a
narrative; they exist, rather, as a group of anecdotes
which are told among a group of camp men until the
story-teller of the gang is started on a narrative which
he makes up as he yarns along, and which may take
him an hour, or three evenings, to relate. A Paul
Bunyan bunkhouse service is a glory to hear, when it
is spontaneous and in a proper setting; preferably
around a big heater in the winter, when the wind is
howling through crackling boughs outside, and the
pungent smell of steaming wool drifts down from the
drying lines above the stove. When the vasty spirit
of the woods really moves the meeting a noble and
expansive ecstasy of the soul is exhibited. Remarks
are passed about a similar night in Paul Bunyan's
camp, when the wind blew so hard that Big Ole, the
blacksmith, had to bolt iron straps over the logs to
keep them from being sucked up the chimneys. The
theme grows and bears strange fruits; and finally the
camp bard harvests them all in a story based on such
a venerable anecdote as that one about Big Ole toting
one of Babe's ox shoes for half a mile and sinking knee-
deep into the solid rock at every step.

This anecdote is what might be called a "key story,"
for it is one of the very old ones. There are at least

a hundred of these, all familiar to every man who has worked long in the woods. They all deal with some of the characters whom tradition has placed about Paul Bunyan, with the mighty logger himself as the main hero; their settings are in such regions as the Onion River country, the Bullfrog Lake country, or the Leaning Pine country; and each one is a theme for gorgeous yarns, when a knowing and gifted camp bard is inspired to use it.

Nowadays, with a shed garage in every logging camp, a radio in the camp office, graphophones in the bunkhouses, and a jazz shack in the village just "over the hump," the camp bard has a scant audience. But in happier times each camp enjoyed its chief story-teller; and such a bard could take one of the key stories and elaborate on it for hours, building a complete narrative, picturing awe-inspiring characters, inventing dialogue of astonishing eloquence. (And what stupendous curses, terrifying threats and verbose orations such bards as Happy Olsen and Old Time Sandy could invent!) It is the method of the old bards that I have attempted to follow in writing this book.

The art of the plain American, which in the last century brought forth tales and songs as native to the soil as the grass of the prairies, is at last perishing under the feet of the herd arts of a perfected democratic culture. The legends about Buffalo Bill and Brigham Young have passed; these heroes are now plain figures in book history. Jim Bridger, the heroic "old man of the mountains," is obscenely and falsely portrayed in a movie to draw snickers from the chiropractors, pants salesmen and tin-roofers who are the passionate devotees of this carnal herd art. Kentucky and Tennessee mountain folk still tell their tales about "ol' Dan'l, tales in which the listener will discover a Boone a thousand times more picturesque and grand than the hero of written history. Crockett, Carson, old Andy Jackson, Sam Houston—but I could name a score whom the plain man's untutored art ennobled and glorified in a manner that put the erudite narrators to shame. This art is perishing simply because Universal Education, and other blights, curses and evil inventions of democracy are destroying all the old simplicity, imaginativeness and self-amusement of plain American life.

Only in a few regions, and among the elders, do the creations of this art, this folk lore, or whatever one wills to call it, survive as shining memorials to sturdier and nobler days. And the legend of Paul Bunyan is certainly the greatest of these creations; for it embodies the souls of the millions of American camp men who have always done the hard and perilous pioneer labor of this country. It is true American legend now, for Paul Bunyan, as he stands to-day, is absolutely American from head to foot. He visualizes perfectly the American love of tall talk and tall doings, the true American exuberance and extravagance. Beginning in Paul Bunyon, soldier with Papineau, he has become the creation of whole generations of men. Thousands of narrators by far-flung campfires have contributed their mites to the classical picture of him. And he, at least, will live as long as there is a forest for his refuge, as long as there are shadows and whispers of trees.

I want to thank the old camp comrades who have sent me so many versions of all the known key stories, and who have given me accounts of new ideas. They, and several lumbermen also, have been very kind to me. And I owe gratitude particularly to Mr. H. L. Mencken, of the *American Mercury*. Without his help and encouragement the stories would not have been written.

PAUL BUNYAN

THE WINTER OF THE
BLUE SNOW

PAUL BUNYAN was the one historian of the useful and the beautiful; other writers of history tell only of terrible and dramatic events. Therefore the chronicles of Paul Bunyan, the mighty logger, the inventor of the lumber industry, the leader-hero of the best band of bullies, the finest bunch of savages, that ever tramped the continent, the master orator of a land that has since grown forests of orators—his chronicles alone tell of the Winter of the Blue Snow.

The blue snow fell first in the North. It fell scantily in its earlier hours, its sapphire flakes floating down on the waves of a mild winter wind, and glittering in an ashen gold light, a sober pale radiance which shimmered through silver mists. There was poetry in the spectacle of these hours. And then the hard gray ground of a peopleless land was hidden under a blanket of dark blue. And the nameless frozen lakes and rivers, the silent valleys and the windy hills of the country were all spread over with a sky-dyed snow. When the last light of this day went out, the boughs of the great pines were creaking under heavy wet masses of snow like torn bales of blue cotton. There was a rush in the snowfall now, as a fiercer wind whipped it on; its heavy flakes were driven down in thick, whirling clusters, in streaming veils, leaping lines and dashing columns; and there were cloudlike swarms of the blue flakes, which settled slowly, floating easily in the hard wind. This wind got so strong that it shivered the timber, and the piles of blue snow which had gathered on the pine boughs were shaken down. Most of this snow fell into blue mounds around the trees, but some of it fell on the fauna of the forest, adding to their troublement.

At the time of the Winter of the Blue Snow, the forest creatures of this land lived a free and easy life. Man was not there to embarrass them with accusations of trespass and to slay them for their ignorance of the crime. Their main problem was the overcrowding of the forests. The vast moose herds, who populated the woods so densely that traffic through their favorite timber was dangerous, made the matter of getting food a simple one for the carnivorous animals. There were many moose to spare, and the elders of the herds, like most prolific parents, never became frantically resentful over the loss of an offspring. The moose themselves, of course, lived easily on the crisp, juicy moose grass which grew so plenteously in these regions before the blue snow. So the carnivorous creatures of the forests lived a fast and furious life; and it is certain that if they were capable of praise, they had good praises for the moose meat which they got with such little difficulty. The coal-black bruins of the North were an especially happy crowd. Theirs was a gay, frolicsome life in the summer time, when the big bruins danced and galloped through sunny valleys and the small ones had rolling races on shady hill-

sides. In the fall, all fat and drowsy from moose
meat, the bruins would go to sleep in their warm caves
and dream pleasantly all winter.

They were all dreaming now; and the blue snow
would no doubt have fallen and melted away without
their knowledge had it not been for the moose herds
which crowded the forest aisles. Moose at that time
did not have it in them to enjoy wonder, and they had
not learned to combat fear, for they were never afraid.
Still, they had some imagination, and the moose
trembled when the first blue snowflakes fell among
them. They kept up an appearance of unconcern at
first, eating moose moss as usual; but they sniffed
gingerly at the blue streaks in it, and they stole furtive
glances at each other as they bravely ate. This
strange snowfall was certainly breeding fear of it in
the hearts of all the moose, but each one seemed determined to be the last one to show it. However, as
the day-end got near, and the wind grew more boisterous, shaking snow masses from the trees, some of
the moose had fits of trembling and eye-rolling which
they could not conceal. When a heap of snow
dropped on the back of some timid moose, he would
twist his head sharply and stare with bulging eyes at
the mysteriously fearsome color, then he would prance
wildly until the unwelcome snow was bucked from his
shivering back. When the early shadows of evening
came among the trees, the moose all had a heavy darkness of fear in their hearts. Little was needed to put
them in a panic.

It was a great bull moose, a herd king, who forgot

the example he owed to his weaker kindred and unloosed a thunderous bellow of terror which started the
moose flight, the first memorable incident of the Winter of the Blue Snow. An overladen bough cracked
above him; it fell and straddled him from quivering
tail to flailing horns, burying him under its wet blue
load. He reared out roaring, and his own herd echoed
the cry; then a storm of moose bellows crashed through
the forest. This tumult died, but there followed the
earth-shaking thunder of a stampede.

The bruins, awakened from their pleasant dreams,
came out from their caves and blinked at the hosts of
terrified moose which were galloping past. The earth-
shaking uproar of the flight at last thoroughly aroused
the bruins, and they began to sniff the air uneasily.
Then they noticed the blue snow; and now in front
of every cave crowds of bruins were staring down at
the snow; and each bruin was swaying heavily, lifting
his left front foot as he swayed to the right, and lifting
his right front foot as he swayed to the left. The
bruins had no courage either, and, once they had got
sleep out of their heads, nearly all of them took out
after the moose herds. The wind roared louder with
every passing minute this night. And the flakes of the
blue snow were as dense as the particles of a fog. At
dawn a blue blizzard was raging. But the fauna of
the forest plunged tirelessly on, seeking a refuge of
white snow.

And Niagara, made faithless by the Blue Terror,
galloped behind them—Niagara, the great moose

hound, bread-winner for the student of history, Paul Bunyon (his real name), and his companion also.

Paul Bunyon lived at Tonnere Bay.   He dwelt in a cave that was as large as ten Mammoth Caves and which had a roof loftier than any tower or spire.   But this cave was none too vast for Paul Bunyon, the one man of this region, but one man as great as a city of ordinary men.   His tarpaulins and blankets covered one-fourth of the cave floor; his hunting clothes, traps and seines filled another quarter; and the rest of the space was occupied by a fireplace and his papers and books.

For Paul Bunyon was a student now.   There had been a time when he had gone forth in the hunting and fishing season to gather the huge supplies of provender which he required, but now his days and nights were all spent with his books.   Paul Bunyon's favorite food was raw moose meat, and after he found Niagara in the Tall Wolf country he no longer needed to hunt. Each night Niagara trotted out in the darkness and satisfied his own hunger, then he carried mouthfuls of moose to the cave until he had a day's supply of meat for his master.   Niagara was ever careful not to frighten the moose herds; he hunted stealthily and with quiet.   The moose at night were only conscious of a dark cloud looming over them, then numbers of the herds would disappear without painful sound. The moose, if they had thought about it, would have been only thankful to Niagara for lessening the congestion of the forests.

So Paul Bunyon fared well on the moose meat which Niagara brought him, and he lived contentedly as a student in his cave at Tonnere Bay. Each day he studied, and far into the night he figured. Taking a trimmed pine tree for a pencil, he would char its end in the fire and use the cave floor for a slate. He was not long in learning all the history worth knowing, and he became as good a figurer as any man could be.

Vague ambitions began to stir in his soul after this and he often deserted his studies to dream about them. He knew he would not spend his days forever in the cave at Tonnere Bay. Somewhere in the future a great Work was waiting to be done by him. Now it was only a dream; but he was sure that it would be a reality; and he came to think more and more about it. The books were opened less and less; the pine tree pencil was seldom brought from its corner. Paul Bunyon now used another pine tree which still had its boughs; it was a young one, and he brushed his curly black beard with it as he dreamed. But he was still a contented man at the time of the Winter of the Blue Snow, for his dreams had not yet blazed up in a desire for any certain attainment.

On the first day of the blue snow, Paul Bunyon was in a particularly contented mood. He sat all that day before his fire; so charmed with drowsy thoughts was he that he did not once look out. It had been dark a long time before he rolled into his blankets. He awoke at the dawn of a day that had scarcely more light than the night. He was cold, and he got up to throw an armful of trees on the fire. Then he saw the blue drifts which had piled up before the cave, and he saw the fog of the blue blizzard. He heard the roar of a terrific wind, too, and he knew that the storm was perilous as well as strange. But Paul Bunyon thought gladly of the blue snow, for it was a beautiful event, and the historians he liked most would write wonderful books about it.

He kicked the drifts away from the cave entrance, but the usual pile of slain moose was not under them. Paul Bunyon was a little worried, as he thought that Niagara might have lost himself in the blue blizzard. The possibility that the unnatural color of the storm might send the fauna of the forest, and Niagara as well, into panicky flight did not occur to him. He was sure that Niagara would return with a grand supply of moose meat when the blue blizzard had passed.

But the moose herds were now far to the North, fleeing blindly from the blue snow. The bruins galloped after them. Before the day was over, Niagara had overtaken the bruins and was gaining on the moose. At nightfall his lunging strides had carried him far ahead of all the fauna of the forest. He galloped yet faster as he reached the blacker darkness of the Arctic winter. Now the darkness was so heavy that even his powerful eyes could not see in it. . . . Niagara at last ran head-on into the North Pole; the terrific speed at which he was traveling threw his body whirling high in the air; when Niagara fell he crashed through ninety feet of ice, and the polar fields cracked explosively as his struggles convulsed the waters under them. . . . Then only mournful blasts of wind sounded in the night of the Farthest North.

The moose were wearied out before they reached the white Arctic, and hordes of them fell and perished in the blizzard; many others died from fright, and only a tiny remnant of the great herds survived. Some of the bruins reached the polar fields, and they have lived there since. Their hair had turned white from fright, and their descendants still wear that mark of fear. Others were not frightened so much, and their hair only turned gray. They did not run out of the timber, and their descendants, the silver-tip grizzlies, still live in the Northern woods. The baby bruins were only scared out of their growth, and their black descendants now grow no larger than the cubs of Paul Bunyon's time.

Being ignorant of this disaster, Paul Bunyon was comfortable enough while the blizzard lasted. He had a good store of trees on hand and his cave was warm in the storm. He got hungry in the last days; but this emotion, or any emotion, for that matter, could have but little power over him when he was dreaming. And he dreamed deeply now of great enterprises; his dreams were formless, without any substance of reality; but they had brilliant colors, and they made him very hopeful.

The sun shone at last from a whitish blue sky, and the strange snow fell no more. A snapping cold was in the land; and pine boughs were bangled and bro-caded with glittering blue crystals, and crusty blue snow crackled underfoot.

Paul Bunyon strapped on his snow shoes and started

out through the Border forests in search of Niagara. His was a kingly figure as he mushed through the pine trees, looming above all but the very tallest of them. He wore a wine-red hunting cap, and his glossy hair and beard shone under it with a blackness that blended with the cap's color perfectly. His unique eyebrows were black also; covering a fourth of his forehead above the eyes, they narrowed where they arched down under his temples, and they ended in thin curls just in front of his ears. His mustache had natural twirls and he never disturbed it. He wore a yellow muffler this morning under his virile curly beard. His mackinaw coat was of huge orange and purple checks. His mackinaw pants were sober-seeming, having tan and light gray checks, but some small crimson dots and crosses brightened them. Green wool socks showed above his black boots, which had buckskin laces and big brass eyelets and hooks. And he wore striped mittens of white and plum color. Paul Bunyon was a gorgeous picture this morning in the frozen fields and forests, all covered with blue snow which sparkled in a pale gold light.

That day and the next, and for five more days, he searched in vain for Niagara; and neither did he see any moose herds in the woods. Only the frost crackles broke the silences of the deserted blue forests. And at last Paul Bunyon returned to his cave, feeling depressed and lonely. He had not thought that the companionship of Niagara could mean so much to him. In his mood of depression he forgot his hunger and made no further effort to find food.

Lonely Paul Bunyon lay sleepless in his blankets this night, his eyes gleaming through hedgelike eyelashes as their gaze restlessly followed the red flares that shot from the fire and streaked the walls and roof of the cave. He did not realize that his first creative idea was now struggling for birth. He could yet feel no shape of it. He was only conscious of an unaccustomed turmoil of mind. Wearied with fruitless thought, he at last fell into a doze. But Paul Bunyon was not fated to sleep this night. A sustained crashing roar, as of the splintering of millions of timbers, brought him up suddenly; it was hushed for a short second; then a thudding boom sounded from Tonnere Bay. Paul Bunyon leaped to the cave door, and in the moonlight he saw a white wave of water rolling over the blue beach. It came near to the cave before it stopped and receded. He pulled on his boots, and two strides brought him down to the bay. It had been covered with ice seven feet thick, and the cakes of this broken ice were now tossing on heaving waters. Now Paul Bunyon saw two ears show sometimes above the billows; they were of the shape of moose ears, but enormous as his two forefingers. Paul Bunyon waded out into the waters, and he reached these ears a mile from shore. He seized them without fear and he lifted . . . now a head with closed eyes appeared . . . shoulders and forelegs . . . body and hips . . . rear legs and curled tail. It was a calf, newborn apparently, though it was of such a size that Paul Bunyon had to use both arms to carry it.

"*Nom d'un nom!*" exclaimed Paul Bunyon. "*Pauvre petite bleue bête!*"

For this great baby calf was of a bright blue hue which was neither darker nor lighter than the color of the beautiful strange snow. A blue baby ox calf. For such was its sex. Its ears drooped pitifully, and its scrawny, big-jointed legs hung limply below Paul Bunyon's arms. A spasmodic shiver ran from its head to its tail, and its savior was glad to feel this shiver, for it showed that life remained. Paul Bunyon was touched with a tenderness that drove out his loneliness. "*Ma bête,*" he said. "*Mon cher bleu bébé ausha.*"

He turned back through the waters, and the ice cakes pounded each other into bits as they rolled together in his wake. In thirty seconds Paul Bunyon was back in his cave. He spread out his blankets in front of the fire, and he laid Bébé upon them.

Through the night Paul Bunyon worked over the blue ox calf, nursing him back to warm life; and in the morning Bébé was breathing regularly and seemed to rest. Paul Bunyon leaned over to hear his exhalations, and the blue ox calf suddenly opened his mouth and caressed Paul Bunyon's neck with his tongue. Paul Bunyon then discovered that he was ticklish in this region, for the caress impelled him to roll and laugh. The serious student Paul Bunyon had never laughed before; and he now enjoyed the new pleasure to the utmost.

"*Eh, Bébé!*" he chuckled. "*Eh, Bébé! Sacre bleu! Bon bleu, mon cher!*" Bébé raised his eyelids with astonishment upon hearing this cave-shaking chuckle, revealing large, bulging orbs which were of even a heavenlier blue than his silken hair. Such affection and intelligence shone in his eyes that Paul Bunyon wished he would keep his eyes opened. But Bébé was weary and weak, and he closed them again.

He is hungry, thought Paul Bunyon; and he went out to find him food. None of the animals he knew about could supply milk for such a calf as this blue Bébé. But he was newborn and his parents should be somewhere in the neighborhood. Paul Bunyon stepped up on the cliff over which Bébé had bounced when he fell into Tonnere Bay. From here a wide swath of smashed timber ran straight up the side of the tallest Northern mountain. It was here that Bébé had made his thunderous roll of the night before.

Six strides brought Paul Bunyon to the mountain-top. One of its jagged peaks was broken off, showing where Bébé had stumbled over it and fallen. Then Paul Bunyon followed the calf tracks down the land side of the mountain. For two hours he trailed them, but they grew fainter as he went on, and in the Big Bay country the last fall of the blue snow had covered them. Paul Bunyon now had no doubt that Bébé's mother had been frightened by the strange color of the snow and that his blueness was a birthmark. Like Niagara and the fauna of the forest, the parents had stampeded, forgetting the little one. It was no use to search for them.

Paul Bunyon circled back through the forest and gathered a great load of moose moss before he re-

turned to the cave.   This rich food would meet the
lack of milk.   Bébé was asleep before the fireplace
when Paul Bunyon returned, and he still slumbered
while his friend prepared him some moose moss soup.
But when a kettle full of steaming odorous food was
set before him, he opened his eyes with amazing energy and sat up.   It was then that Bébé first showed
the depth and circumference of his natural appetite,
an appetite which was to have its effect on history.
He drank most of the moose moss soup at three gulps,
he seized the rim of the kettle in his teeth and tilted
it up until even the last ten gallons were drained out
of it; then, looking roguishly at Paul Bunyon the
while, he bit off a large section of the kettle rim and
chewed it down, switching his pretty tail to show his
enjoyment.

"*Eh, Bébé!*" roared Paul Bunyon, doubling up with
laughter for the second time in his life.   And he
praised the blue snow for giving him such a creature,
and did not mourn Niagara, who had never been amusing.   But now, as Paul Bunyon doubled over for another rare roar of laughter, he got one more surprise.
He was struck with terrific force from the rear and
knocked flat.   Paul Bunyon hit the cave floor so hard
that its walls were shaken, and a cloud of stones
dropped from the roof, covering him from his hips
to his thighs.   Paul Bunyon dug himself out with no
displeasure.   He was marveling too much to be wrathful.

There is strength in this baby animal, he thought;
surely he has the muscle and energy for great deeds;

for that was such a tremendous butting he gave me that I am more comfortable standing than sitting. So he stood and admired this strong and energetic ox calf, who was calmly seated on his haunches before the fireplace, now throwing his head to the right as he licked his right shoulder, now throwing his head to the left as he licked his left shoulder. While Paul Bunyon admired, he pondered; then, even as Bébé had given him his first laugh, the ox calf now showed him the outline of his first real idea. The thought struck him that his student's life was finally over; there was nothing more for him to learn; there was everything for him to do. The hour for action was at hand.

Indeed, if he was to keep this blue ox calf, action was truly necessary. Bébé had shown that his superabundance of vitality made him dangerous as well as delightful and amusing. This inexhaustible energy of his must be put to work; this vast store of power in an ox-hide should be developed and harnessed to give reality to some one of Paul Bunyon's vague dreams.

Soon the well-fed blue ox calf lay down and slept contentedly. But Paul Bunyon did not sleep. One after another, occupations, enterprises and industries which would be worthy of his knowledge and his extraordinary mental and physical powers, and which would also offer labor great enough for Bébé when he was grown, were considered by Paul Bunyon; but nothing that he thought about satisfied him in the least. Certainly he would have to invent something new; and as he thought of invention, his imagination blazed up like a fire in a dry forest. He was so unused to it that it got out of control, and its smoky flames hid his idea rather than illuminating it.

Wearied at last, he lay on his side, for he remembered his bruises, and he fell into a troubled doze. Now he dreamed and saw great blazing letters which formed the words REAL AMERICA. He sat up, and his bruises gave him such sudden pain that the dream vanished utterly. But he dreamed again before morning. In this second dream he saw no words, but a forest. A flame like a scythe blade sheared through the trees and they fell. Then Paul Bunyon saw in his dream a forest of stumps, and trees were fallen among them.

For many days Paul Bunyon thought about these dreams as he gathered moose moss for Bébé and seined fish from the bay for himself. And for many nights he tried to dream again, but his sleep was the untroubled sleep of the weary.

Bébé grew wonderfully as the weeks went by, and the moose moss made him saucy as well as fat. His bulging blue eyes got a jovial look that was never to leave them. His bellow already had bass tones in it. He would paw and snort and lift his tail as vigorously as any ordinary ox ten times his age. His chest deepened, his back widened, muscle-masses began to swell and quiver under the fat of his shoulders and haunches. The drifts of the beautiful unnatural snow melted away in streams of blue water, and the marvelous color of this historical winter vanished, but the glittering blue of Bébé's silken hair remained. His tail brush was of a darker blue; it looked like a

heavily foliaged cypress bough in purple twilight; and
Bébé was proud of this wonderful tail brush that belonged to him, for he would twist it from behind him
and turn his head and stare at it by the hour.

Now spring came and Paul Bunyon determined to
start out with his blue ox calf and try to find the
meanings of his dreams.   The bright warm hours of
these days gave him a tormenting physical restless-
ness; and his imagination ranged through a thousand
lands, playing over a thousand activities.   It was certainly the time to begin a Life Work.

Each day Paul Bunyon pondered his two dreams
without finding substantial meaning in them.   The
first one indicated that he should go to Real America;
and this Paul Bunyon finally resolved to do, hoping
that he would discover the Work that was meant for
him and the blue ox calf.   He knew that he could not
fare worse in that land, for few of the fauna of his
native country had returned with the spring, and
Paul Bunyon could not live well on a fish diet.
Bébé's growing appetite, too, made some move a
necessity, for the blue snow had killed the moose grass,
and moose moss was a dry food without nourishment
in the summer.   The more Paul Bunyon thought
about Real America, the better he liked the idea of
going there.   Moose and grass, at least, were to be
found across the Border.   And no doubt Real America
was his Land of Opportunity.

So one fine day Paul Bunyon and Bébé came down
to the Border.   The blue ox calf frolicked with his

master and bellowed happily when he saw the green grass and clover on the hills of Real America. He was for rushing over at once, but Paul Bunyon, the student, was not unmindful of his duty to his new country; he would not enter it without fitting ceremonies and pledges, though Bébé butted him soundly in resenting the delay.

Now Paul Bunyon lifted his hands solemnly and spoke in the rightful language of Real America.

"In becoming a Real American, I become Paul *Bunyan*," he declared. "I am Paul *Bunyon* no more. Even so shall my blue ox calf be called Babe, and Bébé no longer. We are now Real Americans both, hearts, souls and hides."

After uttering these words with feeling and solemnity, an emotion more expansive, more uplifting and more inspiring than any he had ever known possessed Paul Bunyan and transfigured him. His chest swelled, his eyes danced and glittered, and his cheeks shone rosily through the black curls of his beard.

"And I'm glad of it!" he roared. "By the holy old mackinaw, and by the hell-jumping, high-tailed, fuzzy-eared, whistling old jeem cris and seventeen slippery saints, I'm *proud* of it, too! Gloriously proud!"

Then he felt amazed beyond words that the simple fact of entering Real America and becoming a Real American could make him feel so exalted, so pure, so noble, so good. And an indomitable conquering spirit had come to him also. He now felt that he could whip his weight in wildcats, that he could pull the clouds out of the sky, or chew up stones, or tell the whole world anything.

"Since becoming a Real American," roared Paul Bunyan, "I can look any man straight in the eye and tell him to go to hell! If I could meet a man of my own size, I'd prove this instantly. We may find such a man and celebrate our naturalization in a Real American manner. We shall see. Yay, Babe!"

Then the two great Real Americans leaped over the Border. Freedom and Inspiration and Uplift were in the very air of this country, and Babe and Paul Bunyan got more noble feelings in every breath. They were greatly exhilarated physically at first; and they galloped over valleys and hills without looking about them, but only breathing this soul-flushing air and roaring and bellowing their delight in it.

But before the day was over, Paul Bunyan discovered that Real America had its sober, matter-of-fact side also. A whisper stirred in his heart: "To work! Take advantage of your opportunity!" The whisper got louder and more insistent every moment; and at last the idea it spoke possessed Paul Bunyan, and he sat down to ponder it, letting Babe graze and roll on the clover-covered hills.

Now the whisper became an insistent cry: "Work! Work! Work!" Paul Bunyan looked up, and he seemed to see the word shining among the clouds; he looked down then into the vast valley, and he seemed to see—by the holy old mackinaw! he did see—the forest of his second dream! And now he knew it: his Life Work was to begin here.

For many days and nights Paul Bunyan pondered on the hillside before the Great Idea came to him. Like all Great Ideas, it was simple enough, once he had thought of it. Real America was covered with forests. A forest was composed of trees. A felled and trimmed tree was a log. Paul Bunyan threw aside his pine tree beard brush and jumped to his feet with a great shout.

"What greater work could be done in Real America than to make logs from trees?" he cried. "Logging! I shall invent this industry and make it the greatest one of all time! I shall become a figure as admired in history as any of the great ones I have read about."

Paul Bunyan then delivered his first oration. The blue ox calf was his only listener; and this was a pity, for Paul Bunyan's first oratorical effort, inspired as it was, surely was one of his noblest ones. But we know the outline of this oration, if not the words. It dealt mainly with the logging method which he had devised in the moment, the one which he used in his first work. So he told of his plan to uproot the trees by hand, and to transport the logs overland, binding a bundle of them on one side of Babe, and hanging a sack of rocks from the other side for ballast. It was months after this that he made his first improvement, the using of a second bundle of logs, instead of rocks, for ballast. And at this moment Paul Bunyan, for all his foresight and imagination, could not have dreamed of the superb tools and marvelous logging methods that he was to originate, or of the countless crews of little loggers that he was to import from France, Ireland, Scotland and Scandinavia, or of the tremendous river drives and the mammoth camp life he was to create. He would have been bewildered then by the fact that he would some day need a foreman as grand as himself for his Life Work; and the notion that he would some day need help in his figuring would have seemed like a far-fetched jest.

No; in this first oration, imaginative and eloquent as it must have been, Paul Bunyan only spoke of simple work for himself and Babe. But he only tells us that the oration was not a long one, for the call to Work came more insistently as he ended each period. At last he had to answer this powerful call. He commanded, "Yay, Babe!" and the baby blue ox and Paul Bunyan descended into the valley to begin the first logging in the Real American woods.

THE BULL OF THE WOODS

"THE straw boss is the backbone of industry," was a favorite saying of Paul Bunyan's. This sage observation is constantly repeated to-day by industrialists who are so overwhelmed by salesmen, efficiency experts, welfare workers and the like that they are forced to leave production in the hands of the powerful race of foremen.

Paul Bunyan had become a true man of the woods, and paperwork troubled him. He was fortunate in discovering the greatest man with figures that ever lived to do his office work for him, and this man, Johnny Inkslinger, did all the figuring alone after he came to camp. But before the renowned timekeeper was found the keeping of his accounts and records was Paul Bunyan's largest difficulty. He figured wearily and the smell of ink often made him sick. His logging operations grew more extensive as time went on. He brought crews of great little men from overseas and organized his first logging camp. He cleared off seven hundred townships in the Smiling River country for a big farm, and John Shears, his earnest boss farmer, managed it so efficiently that new companies of loggers had to be added to the camp each season to use up the produce; consequently, more and more timber was being felled as each season ran its course.

At last it got so that figuring occupied all of Paul Bunyan's time between supper and breakfast, and then he had to take time away from work in the woods for the keeping of his accounts. In vain he tried to increase his speed as a figurer. He learned to write with both hands at once; but this was no use, for the two sets of figures would mix up in his head and result in confusion. He invented the multiplication table, cube root and algebra, but production increased so fast that these short cuts gave him no more time than before for the woods. Then he gave in to necessity and looked about for help. No figurers were anywhere to be discovered, so Paul Bunyan invented bossmen to carry on the work in the woods while he held forth in the office.

His first foreman was Gun Gunderson, commonly known as "Shot" Gunderson because of his explosive nature. He originated the "High-ball System," which is still used in some logging camps. Much of the loggers' tough vocabulary has come down from him. His favorite words of encouragement were: "Put a better notch in that stick or I'll cave your head in!" "Heave harder on that peavy handle, you gizzardless scissor-bill, or I'll put the calks to you!" He began to lose power when the loggers learned his lingo and came back at him fiercely in his own words. His downfall happened in the second winter on Tadpole River, in the Bullfrog Lake country. That was the winter of the Big Wind, which blew so hard for four months that Shot Gunderson had to yell at the top of his voice to be heard in its howling blasts.

His voice cracked under the strain and then, of course, his chief strength as a boss was gone. He became a plain logger again, and Chris Crosshaulsen succeded him.

This industrious man was a worthy and well-beloved boss, but he, too, had a fatal weakness. Such a passion for river driving did he possess that he could never stop the drive at its destination, but he would run the logs on for miles and then drive them back again. This upstream driving was terrible labor, for each logger had to drive one log at a time; treading it, he would roll it against the current. So much time and energy was wasted for Chris Crosshaulsen's pleasure that Paul Bunyan was forced to depose him.

The next chief was Ole Olsen. He was so loved that countless loggers have been named after him, but his tender heart made him a failure as a boss. Other bosses were Lars Larsen, Swan Swanson, Pete Peterson, John Johnson, Jens Jensen, Anders Anderson, Hans Hansen, and Eric Ericksen. They were all noble men, and loggers and mill men are still named in their honor. But not one was powerful enough to keep his job as Paul Bunyan's aide. Once, indeed, it was thought that an ideal foreman had been discovered when a burly man who called himself Murph Murpheson was put on the job. But one night he was heard talking Gaelic in his sleep. Cross-questioned, he admitted that his true name was Pat Murphy; knowing Paul Bunyan's predeliction for Scandivavian foremen he had called himself Murph Murpheson in order to get his high position. Deceit was the one human frailty that the great logger had no tolerance for, and the Irish boss followed his predecessors.

Paul Bunyan was now without a foreman, and he had never had a greater need for a good one. For his next project was to log off the Dakota country, which was then known as the region of the Mountain That Stood On Its Head. Difficulties loomed before him which only he or a better foreman than he had yet discovered could surmount. Unless he discovered either a great figurer or a great foreman success would be improbable.

Then fortune shone on him with sudden, dazzling brightness. For word came down through the woods that the mightiest logger of Sweden was tramping overland for Paul Bunyan's camp. The gossip that ran before him called him Sweden's greatest milker also; and some whispered that he was the greatest fisherman and the greatest hunter of that country of superb giants. It was rumored that he was taller than a tree, as tall as Paul Bunyan and as wide, and that he feared no man. The great logger, toiling over his vast ledgers, heard and hoped that the perfect foreman was coming to him at last.

He arrived at the end of a bright June day. The loggers were at supper, happily occupied with pea soup and hard-tack, which were their only rations at that time. The soup bowls before the loggers were emptying fast, and the cookhouse resounded with a hissing rumble, to which the clangor of the spoons striking the bottoms of the bowls was presently added.

Then above the noise was heard a slow muffled "boom . . . boom . . . boom."

The loggers listened and wondered. "Ol' Paul's walkin' heavy this evenin'," said some. Said others, "But it don't sound like Ol' Paul's step anyway." The booming tramp sounded nearer; the cookhouse began to shake; the loggers, curious and wondering, gulped down the last of their soup and hurried outside.

Through the trees that covered the slopes above the camp they saw a great man approaching. He was not as tall as the tallest trees, but the shortest ones were no higher than his waist. Yellow bristles protuded through the crevices in the hat that was cocked on one side of his head; he walked with a swagger that sent the limbs crashing as he swayed against them; a good-sized pine tree stood in his way, and he cast it aside and marched on. When he had reached the center of the camp he stopped and said in a commanding voice, "Aye wan' see Paul Bunyan."

While he waited the loggers gazed in awe on his heroic figure, and they whispered to one another that here at last was the Swede of wonderful deeds. It was indeed a marvelous moment for them. Every real logger to-day would give ten years of his life to have been among the men who first saw Hels Helsen the mighty, the Big Swede, the incomparable Bull of the Woods.

When Paul Bunyan came forth he made no attempt to conceal his pleasure over the newcomer. For the first time in months the darkness of worry lifted from his countenance and a smile shone through his beard. He shook hands awkwardly, as this was a novel experience for him. Here was a man whom he did not have to look down upon to see, one man who could reach above the great logger's boot tops. Surely he would make an ideal foreman; though a fierce light glittered at moments in his blue eyes, his grin showed that he possessed the amiability that a good foreman must have; being a Swede, he was certainly trustworthy and obedient.

In broken Real American Hels Helsen began to tell Paul Bunyan of the purpose of his journey from the old country. But he got no further than an account of his hard tramp over the polar lands, where he had lived on white bear meat and whale steak, when Paul Bunyan stopped him.

"A mountain of energy, a river of power like yourself does not need to make explanations or ask me for anything," said the mighty logger. "I appoint you foreman at once, without question."

"Fooreman?" asked Hels Helsen, seemingly puzzled.

"Yes," said Paul Bunyan heartily. "You shall be boss over all my loggers in the timber and on the drives. Honor and glory will be yours, for you shall be remembered as long as men fell trees. I will give you a fitting title. I call you 'the Bull of the Woods,' a name which shall be applied to only the greatest of woods bosses hereafter because you were the first to have it."

"Har noo—" began Hels Helsen; but his words

were drowned in the great cheer which had arisen from the excited loggers.

Their enthusiasm inspired Paul Bunyan to make one of his famous speeches. He spoke for an hour about the historic accomplishment that was now certain in the logging off of the Mountain That Stood On Its Head.

"A cheer now, my men, for Hels Helsen, the Bull of the Woods!" Thus Paul Bunyan ended his speech; and the loggers responded with a shout that sounded like one throat had made it.

Several times during the early part of the speech Hels Helsen had attempted to interrupt Paul Bunyan, but he was always silenced by the matchless eloquence of the master orator. And when the loggers cheered him he kept in his heart whatever he wanted to say; he frowned and mumbled powerfully for a moment; but then he grinned and obediently followed Paul Bunyan into the camp office.

The virgin Dakota country of that time had what was no doubt the most beautiful and unique scenic feature in Real America. In the center of a forested plain stood the largest and most original of all mountains, the Mountain That Stood On Its Head. Its peak was buried in the ground, and its slopes ran outward, instead of in toward its summit. It was five miles in a direct line from the head of the mountain and up the slope to the rim of its foot; ascent would seem impossible to any beholder, for a climber up the mountain side would necessarily have to move with his feet uppermost or else walk with his head. The

stubborn pine trees on the mountain sides had refused
to grow unnaturally; they had kept their roots in the
ground, and their tops all pointed downward. The
summit of the mountain (perhaps I should go on saying "foot," but this might prove confusing) was a
plain two miles above a plain, for it was flat and
heavily timbered with the noblest of close-grained
pine. This unnatural but wonderful mountain top
was in the form of a true circle which was one hundred and twenty-seven miles in circumference. At
one place the rim of the circle rose gently, and a mild
slope ran away from it towards the center of the plain.
Here were the High Springs, whose waters formed
Lofty River and flowed smoothly through aisles of
pine and wound among meadows which were abloom
with mountain orchids and fragrant with purple
clover. The falls in which the river made its two
mile drop to the plain below had been named Niagara
by Paul Bunyan, to honor the memory of his old
moose hound, and the name was later passed on to a
little waterfall along the Border.

It was to this place of scenic grandeur that Paul
Bunyan now moved his camp. It was here that he
was determined to try out Hels Helsen and make him
prove his right to the title of Bull of the Woods. The
camp was put in order; the axmen and sawyers were
given their stations in the woods, trails were swamped
out for Babe, the big blue ox, to use in snaking the
logs to the landings, Hels Helsen was given final instructions. Paul Bunyan then retired with a sigh to
his ledgers, and the logging began.

Paul Bunyan had figured that it would require two seasons to log off Dakota; one season for the low lands, and one for the mountain. But he did not know Hels Helsen, the Big Swede. From the time that he yelled, "Roll out or roll up!" on his first morning in camp the loggers felt the urge of a new power and they put a vigor and force into their work which had been lacking for a long time. Not often did the Bull of the Woods speak to them, but when he did his roar made the loggers remember his title; and the chips flew from the ax bits like leaves in a wind, and the saws smoked as they flashed back and forth in the tree trunks.

Logs piled up ahead of the blue ox, but Hels Helsen, remembering the tricks he had learned as a great man with cattle in the old country, took the exuberant, well-meaning creature in hand and taught him speed. So active did Babe become that only Hels Helsen could handle him. Each morning, eager to get to work, he galloped madly for the woods, while the foreman held grimly to the halter rope, thrown from his feet very often, hurled through the air, bounced over rocks and stumps, but holding fast always.

So rapidly did the logging go on that Paul Bunyan could only accomplish the necessary figuring by giving all of his time to it. He began to weary of his hours at the desk, while his soul cried out for the timber; he envied Hels Helsen for the ideal life he was living, but he gladly gave him the honor and glory that was his due. Latin Paul Bunyan praised his great Nordic foreman constantly and said nothing of himself.

Now, as Paul Bunyan's only physical weakness was a ticklishness of the neck, so was his only mental weakness extreme modesty. He never boasted, and he never belittled the pretensions of his men by reminding them of his own part in their achievements. Consequently, his inventions were taken as a matter of course, and his paperwork was not considered very difficult by his loggers because they knew nothing about it. His praise of Hels Helsen, and his reticence about himself, naturally made his men exaggerate the greatness of the Bull of the Woods and minimize the importance of Paul Bunyan.

The effect on Hels Helsen was even more dangerous. In the first place he had not come to Paul Bunyan with the intention of seeking a foreman's job; he had wanted to propose a partnership between the greatest man of Sweden and the greatest man of Real America. But Paul Bunyan's oratory had baffled him, and he had taken the position without arguing for what he considered his rightful place. However, a resentment had been kindled in his soul; and with his success as a foreman it flamed into an exalted opinion of his own powers; as the time for logging off the mountain approached he resolved to not only make this enterprise bring him equality with Paul Bunyan but a position of command over him. Therefore, a terrible conflict was inevitable.

The first intimation that Paul Bunyan had of the coming struggle was during the preparations for logging off the mountain. He himself had made many plans for accomplishing the difficult job, taking time from his office work to think them out. Then the first drive was finished and the day came when felling was to begin on the mountain side. On that morning Paul Bunyan was about to call his foreman to give him instructions when he heard the loggers marching out of camp. Hels Helsen was taking them to the woods; the foreman had seemed to think it unnecessary to consult with Paul Bunyan. For a moment the master of the camp had a raging impulse to take after them and assert his authority, but his good sense restrained him.

"There is no appetite more powerful than that for the strong meat of authority," Paul Bunyan always told his bossmen. "But if you bite off more than you can chew, nothing will choke you more surely."

Paul Bunyan remembered this saying now, and he thought it best to let Hels Helsen learn the lesson for himself.

So for days he made no inquiries about the progress of the work in the woods. He busied himself with his figures and waited. He noted with secret pleasure the bafflement and worry that showed in deeper lines on Hels Helsen's face each succeeding night. The loggers were always utterly weary now when they got into camp; at last many of them were too exhausted to eat their pea soup when the day was done; others went to sleep at the supper table, and they would not awaken until breakfast time. Then the first week's scale was brought in, and it showed only an average of one tree per man for each seventy-two hours of labor.   The master logger chuckled over this, but he said nothing.

On Monday morning, his accounts being in order, he walked over the hump to where he could observe the logging operations.

On the slopes—or under them, rather—of the Mountain That Stood On Its Head crawled Hels Helsen, and he was urging the loggers to follow him. Not an original method had he devised; he was even insisting that the loggers walk upside down and fell the trees in exactly the same style that they used when standing up.   Having been a champion mountain climber in Sweden, he got up the slopes without much difficulty, and he strung cables between the trees. Along these cables the loggers dizzily worked themselves.   Tree-felling even under ordinary conditions is hard labor for the strongest men.   But when a woodsman attempts to operate a limber crosscut saw and a heavy ax, his head down, his body hanging by a leather belt which is fastened to a swaying cable; when a woodsman looks up to see his feet and to have dirt and sawdust fall down in his eyes; when a woodsman looks down to see rocks and stumps a mile and a half below him—brave and powerful though he may be, a woodsman in such circumstances is bound to feel inconvenienced, harassed and impeded in the performance of his labor.   And even the threatening roars and the pleading bellows of a Hels Helsen, the supreme and original Bull of the Woods, cannot make him work efficiently.

"The test of great leadership is originality," mused Paul Bunyan, as he returned to camp. "At least some inventiveness is needed. Herioc Hels Helsen, the Bull of the Woods—a fair title. The hero inspires, but the thinker leads. I shall now think. One great idea put into action can set the world afire. Surely it will take no more than a common one to master Hels Helsen."

In such solemn ponderings Paul Bunyan spent the rest of the day. Until midnight he thought, and then the idea came. He at once went to work to make a reality of it.

From an old chest that held the weapons and traps of his pre-logging days he brought forth the most prized weapon of his youth, a gold-butted, diamond-mounted, double-barreled shot gun. He spent the rest of the night in careful cleaning of all its parts. An idea of the size and power of this super-cannon can be gained when it is remembered that he used its two barrels at a later time as smokestacks for his first sawmill. The shells for it were made from the largest cedar logs in the country; they were hollowed out, bound with brass, and capped with sheet iron.

After breakfast, when the loggers had gone wearily to their terrible labor, Paul Bunyan ordered Big Ole, the blacksmith, to cut up thousands of pieces of sheet iron, making each one two feet square. In two days he had the shells loaded, and he was ready to try out his idea. Then he waited for the time when Hels Helsen would have to call on him for help. And this time was sure to come soon, for as the work slowly moved up from the head of the mountain the un-imaginative logging methods of the stubborn Bull of the Woods could not but fail completely. And Hels Helsen was not the leader to change these methods himself; he was only a hero.

But Paul Bunyan was not prepared for the monstrous display of effrontery which was given by Hels Helsen when the exhausted loggers could no longer follow him up the mountain side.

One morning the foreman did not call the men out to work; instead, Paul Bunyan heard him giving them orders to pack up.

"Thunderation!" exclaimed the master logger. "What means this, Hels?"

The Bull of the Woods was attaching a cable to the cookhouse skids. He looked up with an insolent grin.

"Aye forgot tal you, Bunyan, but aye goin' move dar camp," he said, in tones of marked disrespect. "No use to try har no moore noo, aye tank. Logger can' stan' on head mooch lonker har. Aye don' tank so, Bunyan. We move new yob noo."

"Bunyan!" exploded the appalled leader. " 'Bunyan,' you call me! You think *you'll* move the camp! *You* will do so! By the blazing sands of the hot high hills of hell, and by the stink and steam of its low swamp water, how in the name of the holy old mackinaw, how in the names of the whistling old, roaring old, jumping old, bald-headed, blue-bellied jeem cris and the dod derned dod do you figure you're wearing any shining crown of supreme authority in this man's camp? Say!!!"

"Aye tank so," said Hels Helsen calmly.

"Suffering old saints and bleary-eyed fathers!"

"Yah, aye tank so."

With a mighty effort Paul Bunyan recovered his poise and dignity. He strode to the office and got his shot gun and a sack of shells loaded with sheet iron squares. Then his "All out, men!" rolled through the camp.

The power of that unloosed voice threw each logger into the air, and they all dropped, bottoms down, on the rocky ground. They were still dazed men as they wabbled to their feet, and they meekly followed their rightful leader toward the mountain, rubbing sore spots with their hands as they staggered along. Muttering darkly, Hels Helsen followed at a distance.

Paul Bunyan halted the loggers before they reached the shadows of the mountain. He turned and faced them, and for a moment they stood in breathless terror, fearing that he was going to urge them to another effort on the slopes above. But no. Paul Bunyan only said, in the tones of a gentle teacher, "You see before you a logged-off plain. Only stumps remain upon its soil. I shall make you a forest. Behold!"

He turned and lifted the shot gun to his shoulder and pulled the triggers; both barrels went off in such a violent explosion that many of the loggers again tumbled to the ground. Clouds of dust dropped from the mountain side and blanketed the plain. When the wind had thinned out the fog the amazed loggers saw the beginnings of a new forest before them. The loads from the two shells had sheared off a thousand trees; they had dropped straightly down and plunged their tops into the plain. And there they stood, the strangest grove ever seen by man. The small brushy tops of the trees were imbedded in the ground, and their huge bare trunks were swaying high in the air. Before the loggers had recovered from their astonishment at the sight Paul Bunyan was firing again; and all that day the terrific explosions of his gun, and the falling clouds of dust from the mountain addled the loggers. At sundown he had completed the circuit around the Mountain That Stood On Its Head; its slopes were shorn of trees, and the plain underneath once more had a forest. It was an amazing artificial one, and the loggers doubted if they could get used to it. But it promised easy logging, and when their leader ordered them into camp they went singing. It looked like the good old times were back.

"Now," said Paul Bunyan to his foreman, "the idea has mastered the material. I turn the job over to you. Go to it in the morning. In the meantime, I'll invent a way to log off the foot of the mountain which towers yonder among the clouds."

Hels Helsen said nothing; but he scowled and scratched his head.

In the morning Paul Bunyan was figuring briskly, quite content again, when he noticed a stir in the camp that was unusual for the late hour. He looked out and saw the loggers wandering idly about. They said that Hels Helsen had not ordered them to roll out but had gone to the woods himself. Sensing that a struggle was at hand for the dominance of the camp, and realizing that the powerful and obtuse Hels Helsen could only be conquered by physical force, Paul Bunyan ordered his men to remain behind, and he started after the foreman.

Hels Helsen was climbing the mountain when Paul Bunyan reached the new forest, and he paid no heed to the calls that were sent after him. The climber had his shoes off, and he moved up swiftly by grasping the largest stumps of the sheared trees with his fingers, wrapping his toes around others and drawing himself up like a rope climber. In a short time he reached the rim and, throwing his leg over it, he drew himself to the top. He rested for a moment, then he stood up and began uprooting the close-grained white pine trees, which extended scores of miles before him. A tumult of rage swelled up in Paul Bunyan's heart. So Hels Helsen had rebelled and become an independent logger. If competition had been necessary to the logging industry the greatest logger himself would have invented it. But he knew that equality was an evil thing; a powerful rival was not to be tolerated; for the sake of the grand new race of loggers, if for nothing else, Hels Helsen must be put in his proper place.

Wise even in wrath, Paul Bunyan did not attempt to climb the mountain. He ran to a far point of the plain, then he turned and rushed back with his greatest speed. When he neared the mountain he leaped, he struck the ground with his knees bending for a spring, and then he threw himself upward in a tremendous lunge. His upstretched hands brushed down the slope and started a roaring avalanche. A large section of the rim gave way, and now a large hill stood under the broken edge of the mountain rim. Again Paul Bunyan ran and leaped; this time he made his second jump from the hilltop and his hands caught over a cliff that jutted below the broken rim. Laboriously he drew himself up, he thrust his foot over the top, and after a struggle that sent more rocks and trees crashing down upon the hill, he won to the plain and lay resting for the battle.

A minute had not passed before he felt the mountain shake, and when he rolled over he saw Hels Helsen rushing upon him. The Big Swede's blue eyes flashed like hot polished steel, the gritting of his teeth sounded like the grind of a rock crusher, his hat was off and his yellow bristles stuck up like tall ripe grain on a squat hill. The pine trees rocked and creaked from the wind of his swinging fists. The mighty Paul Bunyan sprang to his feet and received the furious charge as a cliff of solid rock receives the smash of a tidal wave. . . .

The loggers in camp heard a stupendous uproar of battle, and they fled from the shaking bunkhouses. The bravest among them crawled to the top of the hump, from where they could see the mountain. When they beheld the titanic conflict that was raging two miles above them on the flat mountain top they stood like images of stone and stared affrightedly. Around and around the one hundred and twenty-seven mile circle of the lofty plain the leader and the fore-

man fought with all their powers. Now came a
sound like a thunder-clap as Paul Bunyan smote Hels
Helsen solidly on his square jaw. Now came a sound
like a hurricane screeching through a network of
cables as Hels Helsen's hand seized Paul Bunyan's
beard and was jerked loose. For a long time the
struggle seemed equal, with neither combatant suffering great injury. Then Paul Bunyan's shoulders
struck acres of pine trees with the crash of a tornado.
A heaving mass of dust rolled over him, but the daunt-
less leader's head was suddenly thrust above it; the
loggers saw his fist fly from behind him, it squashed
over Hels Helsen's nose, and the sun shone red through
a spray of blood. . . . Balloons and geysers of dust
now rose explosively all over the mountain top, and
heavy gray clouds soon hid the mountain from view;
trees and rocks crashed everywhere on the plain below;
the convulsions of the earth increased in force; even
the bravest of the loggers were at last terrified by the
shocks and blasts, and they fled to camp and hid under
their blankets.

All night the tumult of battle sounded, but at
dawn there was a crash of such shocking force that
it upset every bunkhouse; and then a sudden hush.
The loggers, all shell-shocked and bruised, crawled
under their overturned bunks, but as the quiet persisted they at length ventured outside. The dust was
still rolling by in thick clouds and they could not
see their hands before them. But at sunup it had
thinned out, and ere long they beheld the figure of one
of the fighters looming in the distance. The conqueror

was carrying his helpless adversary over his shoulder.

And this conqueror, this victor in that tourney of the Titans, that battle of the behemoths, that riot of the races, that Herculean jaw-hammering, chin-mauling, nose-pounding, side-stamping, cheek-tearing, rib-breaking, lip-pinching, back-beating, neck-choking, eye-gouging, tooth-jerking, arm-twisting, head-butting, beard-pulling, ear-biting, bottom-thumping, toe-holding, knee-tickling, shin-cracking, heel-bruising, belly-whacking, hair-yanking, hell-roaring supreme and incomparable knock-down-and-drag-out fight of all history was the mighty leader of the new race of loggers, Battling Paul Bunyan.

Tattered, bloody, dirt-streaked, he marched with dignity still. On through the hosts of silent awed loggers he passed, without glancing down at them. He disappeared with the Bull of the Woods into the camp office.

"You're going to be a good foreman now, Hels Helsen!"

"Aye tank so, Mr. Bunyan."

"You *know* so, Hels Helsen."

"Yah, Mr. Bunyan."

And no more was said.

The wonderful mountain was gone, alas; the struggle had demolished it and scattered its majesty in dust over the plain. To-day the Northern winds blow down over the desolate remains of that once noble and marvelous eminence—the remains of blood-darkened dust which are now known as the Black Hills of Dakota.

A MATTER OF HISTORY

THREE weeks after his cataclysmic fist fight with his foreman, Hels Helsen, Paul Bunyan was up and around, thinking of his next move. Dakota, once a great timberland, was now a brown, barren country; its logs and stumps had been covered with blankets of dust when the Mountain That Stood On Its Head was destroyed, and the mountain itself was now only clusters of black hills. The greatest logging camp of all history was situated in a vacant prairie. It was preposterous.

But the mighty logger did not revile fate, nor did he lift his voice in lamentations. Neither did he have words of condemnation for the belligerent audacity of the Big Swede, who, chastened and meek in defeat, now gazed worshipfully on his conqueror. Still wearing the bruises and scars of battle, he limped around his bunk a few times and then said mildly:

"Aye tank aye soon be back on yob noo, Mr. Bunyan."

"We have no job now. There is no timber within hundreds of miles of us."

Paul Bunyan shook his head sadly; but presently consoling thoughts came to him, and then proud joy flashed in his eyes.

"But what does the ruin of a season's logging

matter?" he said cheerily. "We have made history; and that is what matters. After all, industry is bunk; making history is the true work of the leader-hero. And this fight of ours was the first dramatic historical event since the Winter of the Blue Snow. This idea would be a great consolation to you also, but you lack imagination."

"Yah," said the Big Swede humbly. "Aye yust wan' yob, Mr. Bunyan."

"And a job you shall have," said Paul Bunyan with great heartiness. "We will move at once to—but that is something to be thought about. Wherever we go you shall have full command over the blue ox. And, next to myself, you shall be in command over the loggers. Now that there is peace and understanding between us we can perform impossible labors."

For several hours the great logger talked on, and there was more of enthusiasm than of purpose in his speech, for he was still shaken from the knocks and strokes the Big Swede had given him three weeks before. The foreman went to sleep at length, but all night Paul Bunyan was wakeful with troublous fancies and bright but insubstantial ideas. In the morning, when his mind was calmer and his thoughts more orderly, only one of the notions that had come to him seemed worth while. This was the idea of a double drive, one under his direction, and one in the charge of the Big Swede, but both of them side by side. It should make a unique race. There was some stuff of history in the idea.

So Paul Bunyan determined to forget the Dakota

Disaster and make practical preparations for the new achievement at once. First, he inspected the bunk-houses and found that the loggers had set them up and repaired the bunks. Next, he examined the cook-house, and he saw to his pleasure, that the cooks had it clean of dust and that pea soup was once more bubbling on the stoves. Babe, the big blue ox, was suffering from hayfever, and he sneezed dolefully at long intervals, but the old eager, jovial look was in his eyes; they shone like blue moons when Paul Bunyan looked him over.

Satisfied, the master logger returned to his office. He found the Big Swede on his feet, and there was only a slight limp in his walk this morning. It looked indeed like good luck was returning, and Paul Bunyan thought of the double drive with great hope. In a splendid good humor he jested with his foreman as he opened his roll-top desk to examine his papers. But the great logger's merriment was quickly hushed as the desk top rolled up and a frightful sight was revealed. The shock of battle had shaken the ink barrels into pieces, and the shelf on which they stood was now covered with a black mass of broken staves. Below were his ledgers. In dismay Paul Bunyan pulled them out and opened them. Nearly every page was wet and black, and the old figures were almost illegible. The Ledgers from 1 to 7, for example, seemed to be entirely ruined. Ledger No. 1111 had black pages up to page 27,000, and its other sheets were badly smeared. Even Ledger 10,000, the last one in the row, had streaks and daubs on most of its

sheets, and only the last 3,723 pages remained un-
stained. Paul Bunyan was appalled, and only his
brave heart could have kept courage in such discouraging circumstances.

He wished to be alone, so he gave the Big Swede
instructions to groom the blue ox and trim his hooves.
When the foreman was gone, Paul Bunyan sat down,
and, having dug a young pine tree out of the earth, he
began to brush his beard and ponder.

The damage done to his precious records was a
terrible blow, and he thought first of how he might
repair it. As he had said, his main desire was to make
history; his imagination rose above mere industry.
His records contained the history of all his operations,
even to their most minute details, and if no one could
read them his work up to the present time was all
wasted. The loss of his grand history was, to Paul
Bunyan's mind, the most terrible part of the Dakota
Disaster. But his loggers, of course, were only interested in their work; and the Big Swede, too, was
now anxious to show his conqueror that he would be
an obedient, efficient foreman on the next job. It
was Paul Bunyan's duty to find a good one for them,
and one that would make a fitting beginning for a
new history also. Resolving to devote his energies
solely to realizing this hope, he shook off regret and
forced a smile and a jest.

"It is no use crying over spilled ink," he said.

So he put the old ledgers away in the chest which
held his souvenirs, and he brought out a set of new
ones. In them his new records should be made, his

future history written. It should be an account of
splendid deeds and give him enough glory. He found
many gladdening thoughts, and when he gave orders
for a move he showed his men the same cheerful face
that they had always known.

The loggers hustled and bustled, and in a short time
the camp buildings were lined up and fastened together. The grand cookhouse was put in the lead,
Babe was hitched to its skids, and Paul Bunyan and
the Big Swede took stations in front of him. "Yay,
Babe!" the leader said, and the move began.

Happy were the loggers as the camp flew over the
prairie, though not one of them knew where it was
going. All were certain, of course, that they were
headed for some vast timberland where great logging
could be enjoyed. They supposed that Paul Bunyan
planned a surprise for them, as he had not given his
usual graphic and prophetic speech before the start
was made. The word was passed along that the new
job was too wonderful to tell about. But this was
only part of the truth. Paul Bunyan's mind was indeed filled with the idea of a unique double drive,
but he did not yet know where the project could be
carried out. A wide, gentle river with timber on both
sides of it was needed; and once found, he would have
to use his inventiveness to the utmost in order to divide
the stream so that two drives could be made side by
side on it.

Paul Bunyan traveled far with his camp in search
of the ideal river. Powder River looked promising
at first; it was a mile wide, but then it was only a foot

deep. It deepened and got narrow in one place, but this was only a deceitful twist of the stream, for it presently turned and ran on its edge for the rest of its course, its waters a mile deep and a foot wide. Hot River, in the Boiling Springs country, flowed placidly and honestly enough all its way, but it was of a temperature to scald the calks off the loggers' boots. And Wild River, though it was a white water stream, would have served for a double drive; but it was alive with cougarfish, a species resembling the catfish of the Mississippi; but the cougarfish were larger and incomparably more savage and had claws on their tails. Careful Paul Bunyan would not risk his loggers among them.

At last the master logger had only one hope left. It lay in the Twin Rivers country. Twin Rivers were ideal for a double drive, as they were two fat streams which flowed lazily, smoothly, and side by side through a wide valley. But that country was the scene of Paul Bunyan's first logging; it was there that he had invented the industry; and, having no loggers then, he had uprooted trees by handfuls to get his logs. Consequently, second growth timber was not to be hoped for in the greater part of that region. In the lower part of the Twin Rivers valley there might be some new timber, for there Paul Bunyan had taught the blue ox the art of skidding; and he had sheared off most of the trees instead of uprooting them. No doubt there were some new trees on this land, but most of the logs for a double drive on Twin Rivers would have to be procured elsewhere. How he was to get them he did not know. But he was staunch and inflexible in his determination to make the second event of his new history a tremendously successful one.

So Babe was turned toward the Twin Rivers country, and in a few hours the loggers were getting glimpses of familiar scenes as the bunkhouses sailed over stump-covered valleys and hills. They still had no word of Paul Bunyan's intentions, and they were astonished when, at nightfall, the camp was halted at the upper end of Twin Rivers valley and they were told that here was to be their camping place for the season.

There was no moon this night, and from the bunkhouses nothing of the country could be seen except Twin Rivers, which showed surfaces of blurred, tarnished gray in the darkness; they looked like two wide, lonely roads with a tall black hedge between them. Heavy grass was discovered around the camp buildings, but there was no indication anywhere of timber, or even of brush. But the loggers were too tired to wonder; they had been riding for two days behind the blue ox, who could outrun a cyclone, and they were thankful for the chance to rest and sleep.

Paul Bunyan lay in his camp office and listened to the peaceful snores of the Big Swede, who could sleep so well because he lacked imagination. But the great logger's thoughts and visions banished any hope of rest for him. Work should begin at once, and a great idea must precede it. His determination for the double drive was solidly fixed; he *would* get a good plan for it. Now then: first, for a drive there must be logs; next, for logs there must be trees; then, for trees there must be timberland, as trees cannot be conjured from nothingness. Now, all around him was nothing but logged-off land; perhaps it would be possible to invent a way to log off logged-off land. . . . Thunderation! what preposterous notions he was getting! But all his ideas seemed to be as absurd. As the night hours crawled slowly on Paul Bunyan began to doubt his powers. Had the fight with the Big Swede left him a little crazy? Perhaps. At dawn his mind was in a turmoil; he felt that he had brought himself face to face with the supreme crisis of his career, and it looked like he was not to meet it successfully. If so, the meanest swamper in camp would despise him. And the Big Swede—how soon he would lose the humble worship that Paul Bunyan had pounded into him and be filled with a cold Nordic scorn for this Latin victim of imagination! . . . What was wrong with his ideas? Why didn't they swell with their usual superb force and burst into a splendor of magnificent plans? Was this new history of logging, then, to be a history of failure? . . .

In a torment of thought, Paul Bunyan could lie still no longer. Darkness was passing fast now; he threw off his blankets and tramped to the office door. He drew it open, then—motionless, unblinking, breathless—he stared for sixty-six minutes. At last he rubbed his eyes; but then he again stared as woodenly as a heathen idol. He could only believe that his rebellious imagination was deceiving him, that the incredible sight before him was certainly unreal. For he saw trees everywhere; on both sides of the river they reached to the horizon.

They were in exact rows, like trees in an orchard, and each one was a large, smooth, untapering column, flat-topped and without a trace of bark or boughs. Again and again Paul Bunyan rubbed his eyes, thinking to see the strange forest vanish. But it remained, and he rushed out at last and seized one of the trees. He pulled it up easily, and he was more amazed than ever, for it had a sharp point instead of roots. He walked on out into the forest and pulled up others here and there, and they were all exactly alike in shape and size.

So delighted was Paul Bunyan with his miraculous good fortune that for a long time he only walked back and forth among the rows of Pine Orchard—for so he named the forest,—and every moment he found some new feature of it that was wonderful and enchanting. For one thing, he could walk through it without difficulty, as there was room between the rows for one of his feet. He saw that no tedious swamping would be required for the logging-off of this forest—no cutting of brush and trimming of limbs. It would be unnecessary to build the usual trails for the blue ox. As the logs would all be of like size, driving them down the rivers would be play for his men.

At last he tramped back to camp and called the loggers out of the bunkhouses. They came forth groaning and yawning, but when they saw Pine Orchard they too were tremendously enthusiastic about the beautiful logging it offered, and some of them got their axes and saws and began felling at once. The trees were as tall and as large as the medium trees in an ordinary pine forest, but acres of them had been notched and sawn off when the breakfast gong rang. Paul Bunyan, with a cyclonic sigh of relief and content retired to the office to do the first figuring for the new history.

Logging went on at a record-breaking rate during the late summer; early autumn passed, and the loggers still felt that they were enjoying the happiest work of their careers. The Big Swede seemed perfectly contented with his position now; his gentleness and patience with the blue ox could not be surpassed, and he bossed the felling crews efficiently when Paul Bunyan had to leave them to toil over the new ledgers. The great logger himself had not been happier in years, for the logs being all of a size made the figuring simple now, and he spent all but three hours a day in the woods.

With the coming of the snapping frosts of late autumn the operations had reached the lower part of the Twin Rivers valley, and the smooth, bare trees of Pine Orchard were all piled neatly along the banks of the stream. Now the second growth of regular pine trees was reached, and the work of limbing, bucking and swamping again became part of the loggers' duties. But they were fat and saucy from their easy months in Pine Orchard, and the first day's felling in the old-fashioned forest brought down a record number of trees. However, it also brought more figuring for Paul Bunyan, for he now had to keep accounts of a thousand sizes and lengths of logs. This kept him from the woods, though the Big Swede really needed him now because of the problems which develop incessantly in regular logging. Again Paul Bunyan came to feel the need of a great figurer, recorder and secretary; but where was one to be found who had both the size and knowledge to care for his vast bookkeeping system and enormous history books? It was folly to hope for such a man, so Paul Bunyan stuck bravely to his desk and made the best of his situation.

And the logging went on without many discouraging incidents until one morning in November. Then Paul Bunyan looked out and saw that the Twin River next to the camp had risen six feet, though the other Twin was at its normal level. Wondering at the unnatural flood and fearing for the logs piled on the landings, the leader-hero set out at a great pace to discover what was obstructing the flow of the Left Twin. Where the river curved around a cliff he saw what appeared to be a boot as large as his own; it was resting in the stream, and, as it reached from the cliff to the bank between the Twin Rivers it made a perfect dam, and the river had not yet risen to the top of it. Paul Bunyan's gaze traveled up the bootleg and reached a corduroyed knee; then he saw that a remarkable figure was seated on the cliff, the figure of a man who was nearly as large as the master logger.

Remembering the danger to his logs, Paul Bunyan seized the foot that was damning the river and lifted it without ceremony. The released waters boiled and thundered as they rolled on, but above the roar Paul Bunyan heard a voice, soft and mild for all its power, saying, "I beg your pardon."

The master logger could not restrain an exclamation of delight.

"Educated! By the holy old mackinaw!"

He pulled aside the trees from which the grand gentlemanly voice had issued. There sat a man. And such a man!

His long but well-combed hair was level with the tree tops, though he was seated among them. Some black, straight strands of hair fell over a forehead of extraordinary height, a forehead which was marked with deep, grave wrinkles. His black eyebrows resembled nothing so much as fishhooks, breaking down sharply at his nose. His large, pale eyes looked through old-fashioned spectacles. His nose was original; it sloped out to an astonishing length, and a piece of rubber the size of a barrel was pinched over the end of it. He was certainly an educated man. He wore a necktie, for one thing; yes, and there were papers resting on one raised knee; in his right hand was a pencil, and many others were behind his ears. Now he was figuring with incredible speed; then he thrust the rubber in his nose against the paper, shook his head three times and the sheet was clean.

Paul Bunyan wanted to shout and jig like a schoolboy, so jubilant was his logger's soul made by the sight of this marvelous man. Here was the one person who was needed to make his camp a perfectly organized industry, to guarantee the success of his plans to become a maker of history. By hook or crook he must have him.

He tapped the engrossed figurer on the shoulder.

"Paul Bunyan, the master logger, the maker of history and inventor of note, the only living Real American leader-hero of industry, addresses you," he said impressively.

"I have heard of you," said the other, extending his hand but not rising. "I am John Rogers Inkslinger, the master figurer, the one and only Real American surveyor. But you must excuse me now, for I am endeavoring to solve the one problem that has ever baffled me. I have been working on it steadily for two months, and still the answer evades me."

He at once began figuring again, and Paul Bunyan, a little awed, had no words to say at that moment. He had no idea of what a surveyor might be, and he feared that John Rogers Inkslinger was something greater than himself. He would find out. So he said:

"I am a figurer also, though not a great one. Yet I might help you. What is your problem?"

"I am looking for Section 37," said John Rogers Inkslinger.

"Section 37?"

"Yes. I have only found thirty-six sections in each of the townships which I have surveyed here. There should be thirty-seven."

Paul Bunyan was delighted that he could solve the problem so easily. "When I first logged off lower

Twin Rivers valley," he said, "I had no logging crews, but only Babe, my big blue ox. The method I used was to hitch Babe to a section of timber—this ox of mine, Mr. Inkslinger, can pull anything that man can walk on—, snake it to the river, shear off the trees, and then haul the logged off land back to its place. I handled a township a week in this fashion; but I always left Section 37 in the river on Saturday night, and the stream would wash it away. Now I judge that you survey the land as I measured it; consequently, you have only found thirty-six sections in each township."

"Bless my soul!" cried John Rogers Inkslinger admiringly. "I should have looked you up before. But I supposed you were an ordinary man of the forests. You would certainly make a great surveyor. You must leave this common life you are leading and come with me. Together we will soon have every section of land in the country staked out perfectly."

"I have a different idea," said Paul Bunyan.

Whereupon he unloosed his eloquence, and for the rest of the day his richest phrases were lavished on the surveyor. And this man, sure of the greatness of his own accomplishments, listened with strong doubts for a long time. But at last he was convinced that logging was the greatest of all occupations and that Paul Bunyan towered far above him as a hero.

"I can only think of you with awe and admiration," he said at last. "But I have my own work, inconsequential as it now seems. So I cannot become your figurer at present. Think, Mr. Bunyan, of Real

America's uncharted rivers, her unstaked plains, her unplumbed lakes! It is my mission to—to——"

His speech ended in a yell of fright as a monstrous red tongue was thrust before his eyes; it passed moistly over his face, it rolled oozily behind his ear; then he heard a "moo" that was as loud as muffled thunder, but affectionate and kind. The surveyor wiped his face and his spectacles and turned fearfully to see Babe, the ox whose hair was blue as the sky, gazing at him, with a pleading tenderness in his bulging eyes.

"Even Babe wants you to come with us," said Paul Bunyan, his beard shaking in a chuckle. "Such a powerful argument. Now what in thunderation——"

John Rogers Inkslinger had let out a scream of horror that sent Babe galloping back through the timber.

"My instruments!" cried he. "Your infernal clumsy ox has trampled them and demolished every one. What misfortune!" He jumped to his feet and began looking for his books and papers.

"Gone!" raged the surveyor. "That blue devil has eaten them! All of my records, the history of my works—gone! gone! gone! Eaten by an ox! His four stomachs are crammed with them! Gone! gone! gone!"

"Stop that caterwauling," said Paul Bunyan impatiently. "When my ledgers were ruined, I simply observed, 'There is no use crying over spilled ink.' The hero is even more heroic in disaster than in triumph. Be true to your pretensions."

"Pretensions, the devil!" said John Rogers Inkslinger peevishly. "If you had the true figurer's soul you would give me your sympathy instead of unconsoling platitudes."

Then the tears began to fall from his eyes and made great splashes in the river. Paul Bunyan, saying no more, grasped his arm and marched him toward the camp. The two heroes walked silently until they were out of the timber and had started over the country where Pine Orchard had stood.

Then Paul Bunyan said conversationally, "I found a very original forest here. But it offered splendid logging. . . . Thunderation again! What ails you anyway?"

For John Rogers Inkslinger had once more burst into yells of agony.

"My stakes!" he cried. "My surveyor's stakes! Two years' work ruined, utterly ruined! The stakes that marked my section lines—you have felled them all and dragged them all to the rivers for logs! My stakes that were to have stood forever—gone! gone! gone!"

He choked and gasped, he clutched wildly at nothingness, and then he fainted into the appalled logger's arms. . . .

That winter was the only period of his career in which Paul Bunyan knew the affliction of a guilty conscience. It was true that he had not injured the great surveyor willfully, but the fact that he had destroyed another man's work could not be ignored. He had done irreparable damage and for the peace of his

soul he must somehow make amends, devise consolations and give heart balm and recompense. He only
asked that the surveyor make any demand of him, that
he give him any opportunity to do a service that would
make up for the loss.

But the winter long John Rogers Inkslinger brooded
in the back room of the office and would speak to no
one.   Each day regret bore heavier on Paul Bunyan's
generous heart; Christmas was a time of deep gloom
for him; and when the first sunshine of spring brightened the valley, even the approach of the great double
drive did not cheer him.   He had abandoned his
ledgers, and he spent all of his time in the woods; he
had no wish to record the destruction of the surveyor's
work.

The double drive was a huge success, and the rivermen returned from it singing the praises of Paul Bunyan, who had bested his foreman in the grand race.
But the great logger himself had only cheerless
thoughts as he came to the camp office.   Another
move must now be made, and the sad business of re-
paying John Rogers Inkslinger must be attended to
at last.   He would place his camp and crew, his foreman and the great blue ox, himself and all his august talents unreservedly at the surveyor's disposal.
Better long years of surveying than to leave this blot
on his history.   It would be wretched work for him
and his men, he mused unhappily, as he opened the
office door, but he could not oppose conscience.   His
mind formed the words of a contrite, submissive
speech, he tramped on into the office and prepared to

utter them; then out of the back room rushed John Rogers Inkslinger; his eyes were shining, his face was flushed with happiness, his hands were raised as though in appeal.

"Paul Bunyan, greatest of Real Americans!" he cried. "I have read your histories, and in the pages of them I have learned the grandeur and glory of your deeds, the extent and influence of your power, the might of your mind! I now know your inventiveness, your heroism, your majestic thoughts, your generous heart! To think that I roared about Paul Bunyan using my miserable stakes! And still you smile upon me! Oh, Glory! I beg pardon humbly and ask only to serve you henceforth in your enterprises——"

"Here now," said Paul Bunyan, dumfounded, incredulous of his hearing, greatly embarrassed. "How could you have read my ink-soaked ledgers?"

John Rogers Inkslinger answered him by bringing out one of the volumes and opening it. On the black pages were figures and letters of white; with white ink the great figurer had painstakingly traced out the old dimmed entries, and now every volume was as readable as it had ever been.

"There!" he declaimed. "There, Mr. Bunyan, is the proof of my worth and zeal. I found the ledgers, and when you were on the drive I traced out their messages. From them I learned to worship you. Give me a desk and let me serve you as well hereafter."

Overcome by emotion, Paul Bunyan turned and stared unseeingly at the lands which had once been Pine Orchard. Visions of tremendous accomplishments swept before him; he now had the perfect organization he had always dreamed about, and there could be no good reason for another failure. But he had a new responsibility also; he was now more deeply in debt to this man than ever. For, even as his fists and feet had won him the faith and loyalty of the Big Swede, so had his mind and heart, as revealed in his history, won the extravagant devotion of the greatest figurer. Only mighty works would keep it. Well, he should not fail. Resolutely he faced the unfortunate surveyor, the restorer of ruined accounts, the man who should win fame with him as the greatest figurer of all time.

"Timekeeper Johnny Inkslinger," he said, "shake hands."

THE SOURDOUGH DRIVE

POLITICAL campaigns remind old loggers of the violent debate that once raged between Paul Bunyan, the originator of the lumber industry, and his timekeeper, Johnny Inkslinger. This debate was strictly about business, however, for there was no politics in those days. It was poor policy, argued the timekeeper, to increase the varieties and quantities of edibles grown on Paul Bunyan's great farm simply to make more stuffing for the loggers. He recommended that the camp rations be cut down and that ships be built, in which surplus farm produce could be shipped to European markets. Johnny Inkslinger was the original efficiency expert and he had hordes of figures at hand to support his arguments. Paul Bunyan listened with his usual calm and dignity, brushing his beard with a fresh pine tree and nodding gravely, until the timekeeper began to insist that the loggers could do their work well enough on pea soup and sourdough biscuits; then the great man erupted.

"Good glory, Johnny!" he exclaimed. "Have you forgotten the Sourdough Drive?"

"I have not, Mr. Bunyan," Inkslinger retorted spiritedly. "But I have figures which show you should have handled it differently."

"The hell you have!" roared Paul Bunyan, in rare

tones of anger. "Damn figures and figuring men!"

"And damn a man who damns figures!" thundered Johnny Inkslinger, himself getting angry.

Whereupon Paul Bunyan damned him again in return, and they kept up a furious argument until the trees began to fall among the bunkhouses. The sourdough drive was a subject that tormented Paul Bunyan's feelings whenever he thought of it; it was always a sore spot with him. But when he heard the trees tumbling down in the valley he remembered his dignity and he silenced his timekeeper with a majestic gesture. Then he gave instructions for a Sunday feast so huge and diversified that Hot Biscuit Slim, the chief cook, went into a solemn trance of joy upon receiving the order. The timekeeper could not hide his mortification, and Paul Bunyan clapped him on the shoulder, saying cheerily, "There, there, my lad. You live in a world of figures. I could not expect you to know the soul of the born woodsman. But treasure this always: a logging crew works on its stomach."

After Paul Bunyan had invented logging and brought hosts of little loggers over to Real America to fell trees and drive logs down the rivers, his most baffling problem sprang from the fact that little loggers could not live on raw moose meat as he did. They required cooked food; consequently Paul Bunyan was compelled to build a cookhouse and import cooks. His first cookhouse was a crude affair without any notable mechanical equipment. And his first cooks were men without talent or experience. But Paul Bunyan's loggers were hardy men whose appetites had never been pampered, and no one complained of the camp fare until Pea Soup Shorty took command of the cookhouse.

Pea Soup Shorty was a plump, lazy, complacent rascal, and he made no attempt to feed the loggers anything but hard-tack and pea soup. He even made lunches for them by freezing pea soup around a rope and sending the loggers' lunches out to them in sticks like big candles. Even then the loggers did not complain greatly. Not until the winter in the Bullfrog Lake country were they heard to cry out against their food. That winter Shagline Bill's freight sleds broke the ice on the lake, and the season's supply of split peas was lost in the water. Pea Soup Shorty did not try to originate any new food for the loggers; he simply boiled the lake water and served it to them for pea soup. Then the bunkhouse cranks began to growl; and finally all the loggers revolted against Pea Soup Shorty; and they declared against pea soup also. Paul Bunyan had to look for another kitchen chief. Old Sourdough Sam was his selection.

The Bunyan histories tell that Sourdough Sam made everything but coffee out of sourdough. This substance is really fermented dough, having the rising qualities of yeast. It is said to be an explosive. Modern camp cooks are always at great pains to warn the new kitchen help away from the sourdough bowl, telling them of the sad accident of Sourdough Sam, who had his left arm and right leg blown off in an explosion of the dangerous concoction.

The old cook brought this misfortune on himself.

Sourdough was his weakness as well as his strength. Had he been content to keep it only in the kitchen, where it belonged, and to develop it simply as a food, he, and not his son, Hot Biscuit Slim, might be remembered as the father of camp cookery, even as the mighty Paul Bunyan is venerated as the father of logging. But Sam was prey to wild ideas about the uses of his creation. He declared it could be used for shaving soap, poultices, eye wash, boot grease, hair tonic, shin plasters, ear muffs, chest protectors, corn pads, arch supporters, vest lining, pillow stuffing, lamp fuel, kindling, saw polish and physic. One time he came into the bunkhouse with a chair cushion made out of sourdough. As bad luck would have it, Jonah Wiles, the worst of the bunkhouse cranks, was the first man to sit on it. He always sat hard, and when he dropped on the new chair cushion, he splashed sourdough as high as his ears. Jonah Wiles was fearfully proud of his mackinaw pants, for they were the only pair in camp that had red, green, purple and orange checks. Now the bursted cushion was splashed over all their gaudy colors. Sam apologized humbly and begged the privilege of washing them. His rage showing only in the glitter of his beady blue eyes, Jonah Wiles stripped off the smeared pants and handed them over to the cook. Sourdough Sam recklessly washed them in another of his creations, sourdough suds. Not a thread of color was left in the prized pants; they were a brilliant white when they were returned. The old cook brought them back reluctantly and he was tremendously relieved when Jonah Wiles did not tear into him with oaths and blows. But Jonah Wiles was different from other loggers in that he always concealed even his strongest feelings. So he put on the pants without saying a word, though he was blazing with wrath inside. His rage against the cook was aggravated when his mates began to call him "the legless logger," because of his invisibility from the bottom of his coat to the tops of his boots when he tramped to work. The brilliant white pants did not show at all against a background of snow.

This unfortunate incident led to the important happenings of the Sourdough Drive, which was one of the turning points in the history of logging. For Jonah Wiles now cherished a vicious hostility against Sourdough Sam; with patient cunning he awaited the time when he might be avenged for the outrage that had made him known in the camp as "the legless logger."

Jonah Wiles was not a great man among the loggers; he was only a swamper, and Mark Beaucoup, who was a mighty man with both ax and pike pole, was much more to be feared as a bunkhouse crank. But where Mark Beaucoup was a roaring grouch, Jonah Wiles was a sly, quiet one; he had a devilish insinuating gift of making men see and believe uncomfortable things.

"Too bad yer so hoarse to-night," he would say to a bunkhouse bard who had just finished a song. "I'm thinkin' we're needin' more blankets. Ol' Paul'll let us all freeze to death."

He would lead the bard to think he *did* have a hoarseness, the bunkhouse gayety would vanish and a seed of resentment would be sown against the master logger. Before his pants were ruined Jonah Wiles had never found a grievance which would serve to keep his instinct of revolt always inflamed. But now his misfortune was in his mind constantly. Without openly attacking the culinary methods and creations of Sourdough Sam, he slyly made a terrible shape of them for his bunkhouse mates.

"Poor ol' Sam," he would say, drawing his lean, gray face into an expression of pity. "Poor ol' Sam. He cooks the best he knows how, maybe. But I'm afeard that sourdough uh his'n 'll bring us all to an ontimely end, fin'ly."

Let a logger complain of corns, and Jonah Wiles would remark that he had never heard of corns in the woods before sourdough was invented. He insinuated that everything from ingrown nails and bunions to toothache and falling hair was due to the loggers' sourdough meals. Ere long old Sam was met with silence and bitter looks when he visited the bunkhouses to show a new use of sourdough. And the loggers' appetites fell away; one month after the accident to Jonah Wiles' pants, Johnny Inkslinger joyfully reported to Paul Bunyan that the consumption of flour and soda had been cut in half. The great logger frowned; he had already learned much about the need his men had for good food rightly cooked, though it was no necessity for him.

"But I can't consider this business, now," he said

ruefully. "We've got to get this country logged off before the water drops in Redbottom Lake. When the spring drive is finished we'll settle the feeding problem once and for all time."

Saying this, he thrust a bundle of sharpened axes and two score new crosscut saws into his pocket, and, followed by his timekeeper, he strode for the woods to lay out the work for the next day. Jonah Wiles was then in the kitchen with Sourdough Sam. Paul Bunyan and his timekeeper always walked softly, but the wind from their swinging feet rattled the doors and windows of the cookhouse.

"There they go," muttered Jonah Wiles. "Now listen, Sam. They'll be in the woods for an hour anyway. Now's yer chance to get in good with everybody again. I want yeh to keep yer high place, ol' feller. I've always loved yeh like a brother, an' yer trouble with the boys is grievin' me to a shadder."

"I shore appreciate your sympathy when all is givin' me the cold shoulder," said the cook disconsolately. "But 'tain't no use. Nobody seems willin' to give sourdough a real chance. Folks could use it fer ever'-thing if they wanted to, an' now these fool loggers even hate to eat it."

Jonah Wiles replied with his usual shrewd arguments. Every evening when he thought he had made all the mischievous suggestions to the loggers that it was wise to utter, he would come to the kitchen and, pretending great sympathy and friendliness, he would urge Sourdough Sam into enterprises that could only end disastrously. He was now urging old Sam to dump sourdough into the timekeeper's ink barrels during his absence with Paul Bunyan. The cook had long been sure that small quantities of sourdough would treble the ink supply. But, disheartened and discouraged, he had not ventured to broach the idea to Johnny Inkslinger.

"Make it a surprise party," suggested Jonah Wiles. "Get busy, Sam. It's yer chance to win a real name for yerself."

At last Sourdough Sam yielded to his tempter.

The flunkies had left the kitchen long before. The stoves and cook tables were dark shapes in the twilight shadows. Only the white sourdough tanks stood out in the gloom. Jonah Wiles lifted the top from one of them, and a hissing roar rose from its depths, where the fermented dough worked and bubbled like quicklime. Jonah Wiles beckoned to Sourdough Sam. The cook's eyes shone; he breathed heavily.

"It can't help but work," he whispered.

"Now yer my ol' friend—good ol' Sourdough Sam!" exclaimed Jonah Wiles heartily. "Now yer talkin'. You'll be king of the camp when Johnny Inkslinger finds his ink barrels all full and wonders how it happened. Be the hero yeh really are, Sam!"

"By hickory, I will!" declared the cook.

In a moment he was leaving the kitchen, a foaming five gallon bucket of sourdough in each hand. Jonah Wiles slipped through the shadows until he reached a big tree. There he lingered and watched. He knew certainly that this idea would bring evil on the old cook. The sourdough would ruin the ink as it had

ruined everything else.   But he had never dreamed of
such a grand disaster as befell.   Johnny Inkslinger
had two dozen ink barrels.   A hose line ran from each
one, and when he did his most furious figuring it was
necessary to attach all of them to his fountain pen in
order to get a sufficient flow of ink.   The cook dumped
five gallons of sourdough into the first barrel and five
into the second; then he rushed back to the cookhouse
for more.   At his sixth trip the first barrels he had
treated were boiling and steaming like miniature vol-
canoes.

"They'll settle after bit," said Sourdough Sam op-
timistically.

Vain hope.   No sooner were the words uttered than
a barrel of ink exploded with a dull roar.   The other
treated barrels followed with a blast that sounded like
a salvo of artillery fire.   The camp was shaken.   The
loggers rushed from the bunkhouses and saw a foaming
black torrent rolling out of the camp office.   Sourdough Sam was whirled forth on the flood.   The
bravest of the loggers plunged into the boiling black
stream and dragged him to safety.   He was unconscious, and his left arm and right leg had been lost in
the explosion.   He was gently carried into a bunkhouse.   The head flunky mounted his saddle horse
and galloped after Paul Bunyan.

Jonah Wiles moved inconspicuously among the excited loggers.   A hot exultation was in his heart; he
had never hoped for such a completely triumphant
revenge.   New powers seemed to surge up in him,

too; he felt that he might bring about even greater disasters than this one. But he cautiously repressed these freshly burning hopes and carried the air of a man made dumb by grief. Tobacco crumbs rubbed in his eyes made the tears trickle down his lean cheeks. As the loggers formed into groups and began to speak of the sourdough explosion in doleful tones, they noted the silent, mournful appearance of Jonah Wiles, and, among such expressions as "I was allus afeard sompin like it ud happen"—"Pore ol' Sam, got to be a regular sourdough fanatic"—"Powerful strange, ain't it, the way things work out in this life?"—were heard many words of sympathy for Sourdough's best friend. "Ol' Jonah's takin' it perty hard." "Yeh, you wouldn't think such an ol' crab had that much feelin' in him."

Jonah Wiles heard them and chuckled evilly. They were making his part easy for him. When Paul Bunyan and his timekeeper thundered into camp he was at the fore of the men who pressed around their feet.

Johnny Inkslinger had the unfortunate cook brought into the office, where he had room to work over him. For half an hour surgical instruments, bandages and bottles flashed through his hands as he doctored the cook. Paul Bunyan watched him hopefully; Johnny Inkslinger was not only the greatest figurer but the greatest doctor of his time also.

At last he arose. "He'll pull through, Mr. Bunyan."

Paul Bunyan thanked him and then fell into a profound contemplation of the feeding problem. Johnny Inkslinger wiped the blots of ink from the walls and the puddles from the floor.

"Only two barrels of ink left," he groaned. "How'll I get through the winter, Mr. Bunyan?"

The great logger smiled grimly. "I only wish all my problems were so simple," he said. "Just leave off dotting the i's and crossing the t's and you'll save ink for the necessary writing and figuring. When the spring ink supply comes in you can go over your books again."

"Such a mind!" breathed the timekeeper worshipfully.

But Paul Bunyan felt that even his mind was unequal to the perplexing problem before him. How was he to feed his loggers now? Would they be content with pea soup? Not for long, certainly. Even sourdough hardly satisfied them now. And this dangerous stuff, lively as gunpowder—who would dare to mix, bake, boil, stew and roast it? No sourdough, no work; and this meant another season in the upper Red River country, for he had to be ready for the drive before Redbottom Lake sank to its summer level. Quick action was necessary. Paul Bunyan sent inquiries among the kitchen help for a man who was familiar with the methods of Sourdough Sam. The head flunky reported that no one was so intimate with the old cook as Jonah Wiles, a swamper.

The worst bunkhouse crank came into the presence of Paul Bunyan with confidence that Sourdough Sam, the soul of loyalty, had not mentioned him in connection with the explosion. He presented a sorrow-ful, tear-streaked countenance.

"Be consoled," Paul Bunyan said gently. "Your comrade was performing what he considered to be an act of duty. He shall be remembered with great honor. And I am offering you, his best friend, the position he occupied."

"I'm only a pore swamper, Mr. Bunyan," said Jonah Wiles, in nasal tones of humility "an' I'd never be able to make it in the high job of a cook."

Paul Bunyan stroked his beard with a pine tree, as was his habit in moments of earnest thought. And at the same time Jonah Wiles was glowing with the fire of dangerous inspiration; he had become firmly con-vinced that he was a great originator of damaging ideas. He remembered that Sourdough Sam had a son; the old cook had often spoken of him with parental pride and fondness. With the boy in camp his revenge could go yet farther. Jonah Wiles pounded on Paul Bunyan's toe to attract his attention. The great logger again bent down to him.

"Sourdough Sam has a son which he claims is a greater cook than his dad already," said the bunkhouse crank. "I expect you could send an' get him easy, Mr. Bunyan."

"Where is he, lad?"

"He's down in the Corn Pone country. That's where he's learnin' to be a better cook than Sam, an'——"

Jonah Wiles was bowled over by Paul Bunyan's jubilant roar. Johnny Inkslinger was ordered to set out for the Corn Pone country at once and to return with the young cook, making all speed. The great logger then called his men together and gave them a rousing speech on the need for fast logging, promising them that he would have the old cookhouse going good again in a short time. The loggers cheered him and went contentedly to bed, where all but Jonah Wiles slept with good consciences. But to him the bad conscience was the good one; he rejoiced in evil thoughts. Not a pang of pity did he feel for Sourdough Sam; he had no regrets; he dreamed only of getting his clutches on the son of the man who had ruined his bright pants.

While Johnny Inkslinger was speeding after the new cook Paul Bunyan was struggling with the worst difficulty he had ever encountered. The kitchen was put in charge of the Galloping Kid, the head flunky, for the time being. He was a grand horseman, a mighty figure, as he rode his white horse among the tables at meal time, directing the running flunkies, but he knew little more about cooking than Paul Bunyan himself.

His sourdough creations were all failures; the loggers broke their teeth on them, and what they did swallow was indigestible. All gayety vanished from the bunkhouses; even the bards, with the noble exception of the incomparable, unquenchable Shanty Boy, got silent and morose. Each day less timber was felled. In time the blue ox stood idle most of the day, waiting for loads of logs to be hauled to the landings. A successful conclusion of the logging seemed impossible, but Paul Bunyan would not admit it. A late spring thaw, a great physical revival when the new cook got into action—he stimulated the men with these hopes and kept up some semblance of work in the woods.

Jonah Wiles was now enjoying the happiest time of his life. Everyone was in a state of wretchedness that delighted him. He heard threats of revolt; disastrous events were surely advancing their shadows on the camp of Paul Bunyan; he gloated over the evil he would wreck on the son of his enemy. But he kept his feelings well hidden. His sly suggestions were the source of many of the bitterest complaints the loggers made against their life, but he never complained now himself. His small blue eyes had a watery shine of sympathy for everyone. He spent an hour each night with Sourdough Sam, pretending to console him, but actually enjoying his sufferings.

When the new cook arrived in camp Sourdough Sam was able to sit up and introduce his son to Paul Bunyan—"Hot Biscuit Slim, sir, who's goin' to be one uh the greatest cooks uh history."

The young man leaned nonchalantly against Paul Bunyan's toe and looked up calmly at the mighty figure above him.

"I'll shore be glad to work for you, Mr. Bunyan," he said. "But you'll have to fix things accordin' to my ideas."

"Son, the camp is yours," rumbled Paul Bunyan. "Half of my loggers are now too weak to lift an ax."

Whereupon Hot Biscuit Slim shook his father's

good hand, smiled enigmatically when the old man said, "I'm expectin' you to succeed where I failed with sourdough, boy," and left to inspect the cookhouse. Paul Bunyan and Johnny Inkslinger attended him. When the inspection was finished he had many recommendations to make. He demanded——

A new cookhouse, ten times the size of the present one.

Steam-power, force-feed batter mixers, and a hot cake griddle large enough for a battalion of second cooks to make a line around it.

A battery of great ovens for the baking of pies, cakes, puddings and cookies.

Bins for potatoes and other vegetables.

Fruit and vinegar cellars.

Baking powder and sugar barrels.

Sauerkraut tanks and a frankfurter shed.

An air-tight onion room.

A store of ham, bacon and eggs for the loggers' breakfasts. . . .

"Hold on a moment!" exclaimed Paul Bunyan in bewilderment. "Please tell me first: *what* are hot cakes, pies, cookies, cakes, puddings, ham, bacon, eggs, potatoes, baking powder, sauerkraut, frankfurters and the rest of it?   Can we get them from somewhere, or must I invent them?"

Hot Biscuit Slim patiently explained them to the great logger.

"Holy mackinaw!" said Paul Bunyan, greatly relieved, "I never imagined such things could be.   I'm delighted that they've already been invented."

Hot Biscuit Slim told him that they could all be grown or manufactured on the great farm. Then he went on to recommend that the flunkies be equipped with roller skates, thus tripling their efficiency. He made many other suggestions, and Paul Bunyan agreed to all of them.

"Now to work," said Hot Biscuit Slim. "I'll have a new sourdough dish for the loggers' supper. Sourdough is a contraption that's seen it's day, but I'll make the best of it while I got to use it. Send me your blacksmith."

A unique smell met the loggers when they crowded eagerly into the cookhouse at suppertime, a delightful odor that overpowered the weakest among them. And when the flunkies trotted out, carrying huge platters heaped high with brown, globular mysteries, each one having a curious hole in the center, the famished loggers all bounced about on their benches in uncontrollable excitement, and well they might! For they were being served with the first doughnuts! Doughnut connoisseurs of to-day would have regarded them as crude; they were made from sourdough, they were hard as hickory and unsweetened. But Paul Bunyan's loggers shouted over them; they discovered to their great leader the exuberance and expansion of feeling, the exaltation of spirit, the strengthening of moral qualities, which may develop from grand feeding. As he listened to the extraordinary uproar in the cookhouse and considered it he formed one of his great reflections: Meals make the man.

Jonah Wiles was the one dismal figure among the

feasters. The doughnuts were bitter in his mouth because they were so pleasing to him. He devoured
half a dozen of them and then forced himself to stop,
for he was beginning to feel good-humored. His gaze
turned shiftily towards the kitchen, where Hot Biscuit
Slim was frying doughnuts with astonishing rapidity.
The assistant cooks were rolling out the dough; Big
Ole, the blacksmith, bare-armed and streaming with
sweat, tossed the doughnuts on his anvil and punched
the holes in them with swift strokes. Jonah Wiles
glowered malignantly on the scene. With one meal
the son of his enemy had brought happiness to the
camp and achieved glory.

"He'll learn Jonah Wiles has a few tricks yet," the
worst bunkhouse crank muttered savagely.

After supper he waited for a lull in the bunkhouse
merriment. When it came he emitted a terrific groan.

"I'm afeard them new biscuits with the holes in
'em ain't goin' to set well on the stummick. I'm
afeard——"

"Take yer bellyache outside!" yelled the loggers.

They shoved him through the door and began to
roar out their favorite song, "Jack Haggerty."

"I've still got some tricks," said Jonah Wiles.

He entered the kitchen and greeted Hot Biscuit
Slim with a twisted grin that was supposed to express
sympathy and understanding.

"I'm yer pap's best friend," he said unctuously,
"an' I shore am glad to see yeh makin' sech a fine be-
ginnin' with sourdough."

"Yeh?" said Hot Biscuit Slim.

"Yes siree! An' I allus like to help folks get along, too. I've jist thought uh somethin' new to try with sourdough. Yeh see, the loggers been havin' trouble gettin' inner soles fer their boots. Now if yer pap was doin' it, why he'd jist slip into all the bunkhouses to-night and put sourdough in every boot, fer. . . . Here now, don't yeh go to hit me! I'm a ailin' ol' man, an' crippled, too. What's the matter uh yeh, anyway?"

Hot Biscuit's face was afire with rage.

"So you're the pizen ol' devil what got my ol' man into all that trouble, what nearly got him kilt, what ruint his life!"

He grasped a cold doughnut, swung it far behind him, then hurled it with terrific force at Jonah Wiles' head. It struck him squarely between the eyes, and he dropped without a groan.

"There!" panted Hot Biscuit Slim. "You moanin' ol' hound—you hissin' ol' reptile—you squawlin' ol' tomcat! . . ."

When Jonah Wiles recovered consciousness two months later he discovered the camp in holiday attire. When he learned the occasion of the celebration he was bewildered. He saw the loggers forming in a great crowd on the shore of Redbottom Lake. The water line was low; the spring thaw had evidently come early, for the lake was black with logs. The logging had not been finished before the lake sank below its outlet. Yet the camp was celebrating. Jonah Wiles wondered. Had the new biscuits made the loggers so idiotically happy that no misfortune could quench their spirits?

Jonah Wiles saw that a new cookhouse had been built; the old one was now standing above a rollway on the lake shore. From crevices in its swelling walls, from the eaves and from the chimneys some thick white stuff was oozing and bubbling. "Sourdough!" exclaimed Jonah Wiles, yet more amazed.

At this moment Paul Bunyan lifted Sourdough Sam aloft in his hand that all the loggers might see him. The old cook waved a new crutch at his friends. He was dressed in an amazing fine style; he was even wearing a necktie. He seemed to be the hero of the celebration.

Paul Bunyan now made a speech. He told the loggers of all the marvelous edibles that Hot Biscuit Slim had revealed to him, and he explained in detail his latest and greatest invention, the Big Feed. When the loggers were done cheering Paul Bunyan paid a tribute to Sourdough Sam; the old cook's creation had served a great purpose in the logging industry, he said. Its day was done now, but there remained a last great work for it to perform, a dramatic work that would keep the memory of its creator alive forever. It was fitting that Sourdough Sam should see this before retiring to his old home. Now Paul Bunyan turned to the big blue ox, who was hitched to blocks supporting the old cookhouse.

"Yay, Babe!" he commanded.

The blue ox heaved, the old cookhouse tottered, then

it crashed down the rollway.   A heaving mass of sour-dough rumbled from its cracking sides and surged like a boiling tidal wave over the lake.   The waters began to hiss and foam; the logs were all hidden from sight; the lake looked like a heavy white cloud had dropped into its basin.   The loggers all stared prayerfully; hopeful, yet hardly daring to hope.   Only Sourdough Sam had confidence in the rising powers of his sour-dough.   In Paul Bunyan's hand, he shouted joyously and waved his new crutch.   The great logger himself was not absolutely sure of success at first, but as the tumult of the lake waters increased, he too showed joy and carefully patted Sourdough Sam's back with his little finger.   The leader-hero was pleased to share the glory of this enterprise with such a noble and faithful little man.   Now the waters rose so rapidly that the loggers rushed back in a panic.   In half an hour the sourdough had caused the lake to rise so high that the season's logs were all thundering down Red River valley.   It was a grand day for everyone; but it was the grandest that Sourdough Sam had ever known.

Jonah Wiles was sickened by his enemy's triumph. He contemplated the magnificence of the new cook-house, and he realized that there was now small chance of promoting misery among Paul Bunyan's loggers. The camp could be nothing but a hostile place for him in the new dispensation.   A dejected, baffled man, he sneaked away in his white pants before the loggers re-turned, and shambled over the hills, traveling towards Kansas.

THE BLACK DUCK DINNER

EXCEPT in the spring, when the log drives were being made down the rivers, Sunday was a day of rest in Paul Bunyan's camp. It was a day of earnest thought, and of cleanliness and pleasure also. For on Sunday Paul Bunyan planned the next week's work, thought out his orations, imagined new inventions, and dreamed of historical exploits for the future. And on Sunday his loggers made their beds, cleaned their clothes, and shaved their faces. The pleasures of this day were the pleasures of the table, for Paul Bunyan, after building his second cookhouse, and developing his famous kitchen organization around Hot Biscuit Slim, the chief cook, originated the custom of grand Sunday dinners.

Every Sunday dinner was a feast; but some of them, of course, were nobler and more enjoyable than others. His roast pork and plum pudding dinners always delighted the loggers when they were served on winter Sundays; they shouted over the baked trout and cherry pie Sunday dinners that he gave them in the spring; in the summer a vegetable and strawberry shortcake Sunday dinner made them happy every time; and in the fall the Sunday dinners of fried chicken and peach cobbler made them prance and roar with pleasure. And the Thanksgiving and Christmas dinners of roasted webfooted turkeys, cranberries and chocolate cake—the loggers were always speechless when they thought about them.

Every Sunday morning would see the loggers performing the ceremonies of cleanliness as soon as their after-breakfast pipes were smoked. First, the beds were made; and this was a more trying job than you would think, especially for the loggers who had poor eyesight. These unfortunates would throw their blankets into a pile, then shake them out one at a time, and attempt to replace them in the bunks. Here difficulties beset them, for Paul Bunyan's blankets had small square checks; and it took a sharp eye to detect which was the long way of a blanket, and which was the wide way. Even the most sharp-eyed loggers would sometimes lose confidence in their vision when replacing these perplexing blankets; and they would remove them time and again before deciding that they were spread correctly. As for the cross-eyed and nearsighted men, it was sometimes pitiful to behold the most troubled of them stretching out blankets in their extended hands, turning them in slow revolutions, doubtfully placing them on the bunks, and then wearily lifting them again. These unfortunate men never quitted their Sunday bed-making until they were worn out; and all the following week they were sure that they had the long way of their blankets on the wide way of their bunks. They would swear to have them right next time; but every Sunday their attempts at bed-making would end in as unsatisfying a manner.

Everyone in the West knows that sheepherders of our time often worry themselves into insanity in their lonely camps, trying to discover the wide way and the long way of their quilts and blankets. Fortunately, Paul Bunyan's loggers were all strong-minded men, and their blankets did no more than bedevil them.

After bed-making the loggers heated cans of water over small fires built out in the timber, and they washed their clothes. Shaving, boot-greasing, sole-calking, hair-cutting, beard-trimming, button-sewing, and rip-mending followed; and he was an expert in these Sunday morning chores who had time to stretch out on his smooth blankets for a smoke before the dinner gong rang at twelve.

At the ringing of this gong the inexpressible pleasures of Paul Bunyan's Sundays began. First, the loggers enjoyed the ecstasy of eating; and it was an ecstasy they were fitted to enjoy gloriously. After dinner the loggers would lie on their bunks and dream drowsily all afternoon of a loggers' paradise; and the paradise they dreamed about was none other than Paul Bunyan's camp; but a camp whose life began each day with a Sunday dinner, and whose days were all like the warm drowsy hours of these Sunday afternoons.

But most of the loggers would be awake and hungry again at suppertime, ready to enjoy the Sunday supper of cold meat, potato salad, doughnuts, jelly rolls and coffee. Then in the twilight, and for a long time after the bunkhouse lamps were lit, they would smoke, and talk contentedly of the delight they got from Paul Bunyan's cookhouse; and they would prophesy about the Sunday dinners of the future. There were no bunkhouse pastimes on Sunday nights. After some hours of low-voiced contented talk, the loggers would change their underclothes and get into their newly made beds, rested and inspired for Monday's labor.

The great cookhouse which so ennobled and cheered Paul Bunyan's loggers on their Sundays was the grandest and best planned affair of its kind ever heard of. The dining hall was so commodious and had so much room between the tables that four-horse teams hauled wagonloads of salt, pepper and sugar down the aisles when the shakers and bowls were to be filled. Conveyor belts carried clean dishes to the tables and returned the dirty ones to the wash room. The long-legged flunkies wore roller skates at mealtime, and the fastest among them could sometimes traverse the dining hall in forty-seven minutes.

But it was the kitchen, the powerhouse of this vast establishment, which had the most interest. This domain, ruled by the temperamental culinary genius, Hot Biscuit Slim, was as large as ten Ford plants and as noisy as the Battle of Gettysburg. The utensils that hung on its walls, from the steam-drive potato mashers and sleeve-valve, air-cooled egg beaters to the big armorplate potato kettles, the bigger force-feed batter mixers and the grandiose stew kettles, in which carcasses of cattle floated about like chips in a mill pond when beef dinners were being prepared— these polished utensils glittered even when the ranges were smoking their worst at hot cake time.

Paul Bunyan had devised the monorail system for this kitchen, and overhead cranes rattled about at all hours, carrying loads of dishes from the Dishwashing Department to the Serving Department, loads of vegetables and meats from the Supply Department to the Preparations Department, and loads of dressed food from the Preparations Department to the Finishing Department. The dishes were washed on a carriage like the log carriages of modern sawmills. The head dishwashers jerked levers that threw heaps of dirty dishes from the conveyor belts to the carriage, then the carriage was shot forward until the dishes struck a sharp-edged stream of soapy water that had dropped one hundred feet. The clean dishes were bucked off on live rolls, and the head dishwasher shot the carriage back for another load. Some of the clean dishes were run through dry kilns, and others were piled for air-drying by Swede dish-pilers, who wore leather aprons and mittens and could pile sixty thousand dishes per pair in twelve hours.

A list of the marvels of Paul Bunyan's kitchen would fill a book as large as a dictionary. Elevators whirred between the kitchen and the vegetable bins, and a wide subway held four tracks that led to the fruit and vinegar cellars. A concrete chute carried the coffee grounds, eggshells and other waste to the kitchen yard, and from morning till night it roared like a millrace. Billy Puget, boss over the scraper gang, often had to work his mules and men fourteen hours a day in order to keep the kitchen yard cleaned of coffee grounds and eggshells.

Paul Bunyan's loggers had little understanding of the tremendous organization that was required for the operation of such an establishment as the cookhouse. They thanked old Paul for feeding them so well, and they agreed that Hot Biscuit Slim was a powerful good cook. Less fortunate loggers of to-day think of Paul Bunyan's camp life as a dream of bliss, and they are sure that if they had been there they would have worshiped Paul Bunyan. His own loggers, however, took the cookhouse glories as a matter of course, and they never realized what inventiveness, thought and effort were needed to give them such Sunday dinners and such Sunday afternoon dreams and content.

Nor did Paul Bunyan expect shouted praises and thanks from his loggers. He gave so much to them because he expected much from them. He worked his men twelve hours a day, and, had they thought about it, they would have been astounded by any idea of working less. And they would have been perplexed by any other scheme to ease their lot. If there were not to be great exertions, they would have asked, why their sturdy frames, their eager muscular force? If they were not meant to face hazards, why was daring in their hearts? A noble breed, those loggers of Paul Bunyan's, greatly worthy of their captain! He himself told them in a speech he made at the finishing of the Onion River Drive that they were "a good band of bullies, a fine bunch of savages." I should like to quote this speech in its entirety, for it celebrated the accomplishment of a historical logging enterprise, and it was a master oration which showed the full range and force of Paul Bunyan's oratorical powers. But as nine days and eight nights were required for its delivery, it is obvious that no publication save the *Congressional Record* could give all of it. It was at this time that Paul Bunyan served his great black duck dinner.

The speech ended on a Tuesday, and until the following Saturday morning there were no sounds save the snores of weary men and the scratching of the sleepless Johnny Inkslinger's fountain pen. By Saturday noon he had a time check and a written copy of the oration for every man in camp. After dinner the Big Swede, using a fire hose, a ton of soap, and a tank of hair tonic began to give the blue ox his spring cleaning, and Johnny Inkslinger turned in for the three hours of sleep which he required each week. Paul Bunyan was arranging his personal belongings for the move to a new job and musing on his recent accomplishment. He had never driven logs down a rougher or more treacherous stream than Onion River. And the hills over which the timber had been skidded were so rocky and steep that they tried even the strength of the blue ox. Worst of all was the rank growth of wild onions that had covered the ground. They baffled all attempts to fell the trees at first, for they brought blinding floods of tears to the loggers' eyes and made their efforts not only futile but dangerous. When the Big Swede was standing on a hillside one day, dreaming of the old country, he failed to observe a blinded logger come staggering up the slope, and he did not hear him mumble, "This looks like a good stick."

Not until the logger had chopped a notch in the leg of his boot had the Big Swede realized his peril. Paul Bunyan, baffled by such incidents, was about to abandon the whole operation when the alert Johnny Inkslinger heard of the failure of the Italian garlic crop. He quickly made a contract with the Italian government, which sent over shiploads of laborers to dig up the wild onions and take them home as a substitute for the national relish. When this had been accomplished it was possible to log off the country.

There had been other difficulties to overcome, too, and as Paul Bunyan spread out a tarpaulin and prepared to roll up his boots and workclothes, he remembered them and praised the saints that they were ended. The next job offered the best promise of easy and simple logging of any he had ever encountered. For miles the land rose in gentle slopes from a wide and smoothly flowing river; there was no brush or noxious vegetation among the clean, straight trees; and, best of all, the timber was of a species now extinct, the Leaning Pine. The trees of this variety all leaned in the same direction, and it was thus possible to fell them accurately without the use of wedges. Paul Bunyan was sure of a season's record on this new job. He thought of the fresh brilliancy it would give his fame, and like a row of snowy peaks glimpsed through the spaces of a forest, his teeth glittered through his beard in a magnificent smile. But another thought quickly sobered his countenance. "Those good bullies of mine!" The words came in a gusty murmur. He dropped the tarpaulin and strode over to the cookhouse. Hot Biscuit Slim, the kitchen chief, came forth to meet him. There was a knowing look in the cook's eyes.

"It's to be a great Sunday dinner to-morrer?" he asked, before Paul Bunyan could speak.

"The greatest Sunday dinner ever heard of," said Paul Bunyan. "I want this to be remembered as the noblest meal ever served in a logging camp. My loggers shall feast like the victorious soldiers of old time. It is a natural privilege of heroes to revel after conquest. Remember, as you prepare this feast, that you may also be making immortal glory for yourself."

"You jest leave it to me, Mr. Bunyan!" answered Slim. "If the baker'll do his part with the cream puffs, cakes and pies, I promise you I'll make 'em a meal to remember. First, oyscher stew, an' then for vegytables, cream' cabbage, of course, mash' potatoes an' potato cakes, lettuce an' onions——"

"No onions!" thundered Paul Bunyan. There was a terrific crash in the kitchen as hundreds of skillets and kettles were shaken to the floor.

"Uh—I forgot," stammered Hot Biscuit Slim. "Well, anyway, they'll be oyscher soup, vegytables, sauces, puddin's, hot biscuits, an' meat in dumplin' stew an' mulligan stew, an' they'll be drippin' roasts, all tender an' rich-seasoned—oh, the meat that I'll give 'em! the meat——" he paused sharply, shivered as though from a physical shock, and misery glistened in his eyes—"only—uh—only——"

"Only you have no meat," said Paul Bunyan gently.

"I'm admittin' it," said Slim wretchedly. "Honest, Mr. Bunyan, no matter how I try I jest *can*'t remember to order meat, 'specially for Sunday dinner. I can remember vegytables, fruits an' greens easy as pie, but, by doggy, I always forget meat. I ain't pertendin' a cook's worth keepin' who can't remember meat, no matter how good he is at a fixin' it. I wouldn't blame you if you fired me right off, Mr. Bunyan."

Hot Biscuit Slim leaned against the toe of the hero's boot and wept.

"That means I must rustle deer and bear," said Paul Bunyan patiently. "Well, bear meat and vension will make a royal feast when they have passed through your kettles and ovens. Light the fires, go ahead with your plans; you may yet make history tomorrow!"

He turned away, and Hot Biscuit Slim watched him worshipfully until he was a dim figure on distant hills.

"The best friend me an' my pap ever had," he said. "I'd do anything for a boss like that. I'll learn to remember meat, by doggy, I will!"

Rumors of the marvelous dinner that was being planned reached the bunkhouses, and the loggers indulged in greedy imagining of the promised delights. The day went slowly; the sun seemed to labor down the western sky. Before it sank soft clouds obscured its light, bringing showers and early shadows.

At the approach of darkness Paul Bunyan began his return march to the camp. He was vastly disappointed by the meager results of his hunt. Although he had gone as far as the Turtle River country, he had snared but two deer and three small bears. These only filled a corner of one pocket of his mackinaw, and they would provide but a mere shred of meat apiece for his men. Paul Bunyan did not feel that he had done his best; he was not one to rest on feeble consolations. As he journeyed on he was devising other means to carry out his plans for a memorable and stupendous feast. And ere he was within an hour of the camp the Big Swede was unconsciously outlining the solution of the problem for him.

The Big Swede went to the stable some time after supper to see that Babe was at ease for the night. The clouds were thinning now, and when he opened the stable door soft light poured in on the blue ox, making lustrous spots and streaks on his sleek sides. He turned his head, his bulging blue eyes shining with gentleness and good-will, and his tongue covered the foreman's face in a luscious caress.

"Har noo," remonstrated the Big Swede.

As he solemnly wiped his drenched face he sniffed the fragrance of Babe's breath and stared with a feeling of envy at the clean, glowing hair. When he had finished his inspection and left the stable, it was evident that he was wrestling with some laborious problem. His whole face was tense with a terrific frown; his memory groped among the shadows of some distant happening; he scratched his sides vigorously and breathed deeply of the air, sweet with the odors of washed earth. The purity of the spring weather, the fresh cleanliness it gave the world, and the aroma and sleekness of the blue ox, had brought the Big Swede to face his own sore need of a washing. He dreaded it as an ordeal, an exceptional and hazardous undertaking, and for that reason he wished that he might accomplish it immediately. He wandered aimlessly on, tormented by an unaccustomed conflict of the soul and the flesh, and at last he came to the edge of a cliff. He stared in surprise at the appearance of a lake below. He could not remember so large a body of water near the camp. But the Big Swede had no room for more than one emotion at a time, and a violent resolve now smothered his surprise.

"Yah, aye do him noo," he muttered.

He disrobed swiftly and ran to a rock that jutted from the cliff. Swinging his fists he leaped twice into the air; the second time he flung himself outward in a magnificent dive, his body made a great curve, and then, head first, he plunged downward. But there was no tumultuous surge and splash of waters as a climax of this splendid dive. Instead, the Big Swede's head struck white canvas with a dull, rending impact. For he had mistaken Paul Bunyan's tarpaulin for a lake! The force of his plunge drove him through the canvas and half-buried him in the soft earth underneath. His arms were imprisoned, but his legs waved wildly, and his muffled bellows shook the earth. A prowling logger saw what seemed to be shining marble columns dancing in the moonlight and felt the ground trembling under his feet.

"It can't be," he thought bravely.

Just then the Big Swede made another heroic effort to yell for help, and the logger was shaken from his feet. He jumped up and ran to Johnny Inkslinger with an alarming tale of dancing ghosts that shook the earth. The timekeeper, after sharpening twenty-seven lead pencils to use in case it was necessary to make a report on the spot, started with his medicine case for the place where the logger had directed him. When nearly there he remembered that he had failed to bring his ten gallon carboy of alcohol, which, next to Epsom salts, he considered the most important medicine in his chest. He ran back for it, and by the time he finally reached the Big Swede, that unfortunate's bellows had diminished to groans, and his legs waved with less and less gusto. After thoroughly examining and measuring the legs, Johnny deemed the proof positive that they belonged to the Big Swede. Then he got busy with paper and pencil and figured for half an hour. "According to the strictest mathematical calculations," he announced, "the Big Swede cannot continue to exist in his present interred, or, to be exact, half-interred condition; consequently he must be extricated. I have considered all known means by which this may be accomplished, I have figured, proved, and compared results, and I have arrived at a scientific conclusion. I direct that the blue ox and a cable be brought here at once."

When the loggers had obeyed this command, Johnny made a half-hitch with the cable around the Big Swede's legs, which were waving very feebly now, and in two seconds, amid a monstrous upheaval of dirt and a further rending of the canvas, the Big Swede was dragged out. For a few moments he spat mud like a river dredge; then the timekeeper proffered him the ten gallon carboy of alcohol. It was drained at a gulp, and then, with aid from Johnny Inkslinger, he was able to stagger to the camp office. When Paul Bunyan reached the camp, the Big Swede was lying on his bunk, bundled in bandages from head to foot. Johnny Inkslinger was still busily attending him; bottles of medicine, boxes of pills, a keg of Epsom salts, rolls of bandages, and surgical implements were heaped about the room. The timekeeper gave a detailed account of what had happened, and then Paul Bunyan questioned the victim, who answered briefly, "Aye yoomped, an' aye yoomped, an'—*yeeminy!*"

Johnny Inkslinger gave his chief a voluminous report of the Big Swede's fractures, sprains and contusions.

"He is also suffering from melancholia because he is still unwashed," said Johnny. "But I think I'll restore him. I've dosed him with all my medicines and smeared him with all my salves. I'd have manipulated his spine, but, confound him, he strained his back, and he threatens violence when I touch it. But I have many formulae and systems. He shall live."

"Surely," said Paul Bunyan. "A man is the hardest thing to kill there is."

Knowing that the Big Swede's wounds were nothing in comparison with the ones which he had received in the Dakota battle, Paul Bunyan worried no more about his foreman. He stepped from the camp office, plucked up a young pine tree and brushed his beard, thinking again of his unrealized plan. He remembered the wordless dejection of Hot Biscuit Slim on receiving the scanty supply of deer and bear meat. He determined that the Sunday dinner should yet be as he had planned it; otherwise it would be a bad augury for great achievements in his new enterprise. He thrust the tree into his shirt pocket and walked slowly towards his outdoor headquarters, pondering various schemes that came to mind.

When he reached the white sheet of water he was astonished by its deceptive appearance. It had a silvery glitter in the moonlight, for its surface still held the moisture of the showers. Small wonder, thought Paul Bunyan, that the Big Swede had dived into it; never was a lake more temptingly beautiful or seemingly more deep. He was gazing at the torn canvas and the huge cavity made in the ground by the Big Swede, when he heard a great chorus of shrill and doleful voices in the sky. He looked up and saw an enormous host of black ducks in swerving flight. They had lost their way in the low-hanging clouds at dusk, and now they were seeking a resting place.

Here, thought Paul Bunyan, is a noble offering of chance. Was a black duck more acute than the Big Swede, that the bright, moist canvas would not deceive him also? And once deceived, would not the ensuing dive be fatal? Wasn't a black duck's neck of more delicate structure than the Big Swede's, and wouldn't it surely break when it struck the tarpaulin? This variety of black duck grew as big as a buzzard, and here they were so numerous that clouds of them darkened the moon. Now to deceive them. Paul Bunyan could mimic the voices of all the birds of the air and all the beasts of the fields and woods, save only that of the blue ox, who always replied with a jocular wink when his master attempted to simulate his mellow moo.   In his moments of humor Paul Bunyan declared that he could mimic fish, and one Sunday when he imitated a mother whale bawling for her calf the loggers roared with merriment for seventeen hours, and were only sobered then by exhaustion.   His voice had such power that he could not counterfeit the cry of a single small creature, but only the united cries of flocks and droves.   So he now mimicked perfectly the chorus that rang mournfully in the sky, and at the same time he grasped the edge of the tarpaulin and fluttered it gently.

The effect was marvelous.   Now indeed was the canvas a perfect imitation of water.   Had you been standing by the sole of Paul Bunyan's boot and seen the gentle flutter you would have been sure that you were watching a breeze make pleasant ripples on the surface of a lake.   Ere long the black ducks were enchanted by the sight and sound, and Paul Bunyan heard a violent rush of air above him as of a hurricane sweeping a forest.   A vast dark cloud seemed to plunge out of the sky.   Another instant and the canvas was black with feathered forms.   Paul Bunyan grasped the four corners of the tarpaulin, swung the bundle over his shoulder and strode home to the cookhouse.   Hot Biscuit Slim was called forth, and when he saw the mountainous pile of black ducks that filled the kitchen yard he became hysterical with delight.

He called out the assistant cooks, the flunkies and dish-washers, and, led by Cream Puff Fatty, the baker, the white-clad underlings streamed for eleven minutes from the kitchen door. The chief cook then made them a short but inspiring speech and fired them with his own fierce purpose to make culinary history.

Paul Bunyan listened for a moment, and then sought repose, with peace in his benevolent heart.

All night fires roared in the ranges as preparations went on for the great dinner. The elevators brought a load of vegetables every minute from the deep bins, potatoes were pared and washed, kettles and roasting pans were made ready, and sauces and dressings were devised. The black ducks were scalded, plucked and cleaned by the Preparations Department, and by morning the cranemen were bringing them by the hundreds to the Finishing Department, where the kettles and pans were waiting for them.

Most of the loggers stayed in their bunks this morning, and those who did come to breakfast ate sparingly, saving their appetites. Time passed quietly in the camp. The loggers washed and mended their clothes and greased their boots, but they did not worry themselves with bed-making. The other Sunday morning chores finished, they stretched out on their unmade bunks and smoked. They were silent and preoccupied, but now and again a breeze blowing from the direction of the cookhouse would cause them to sigh. What enchantment was in the air, so redolent with the aroma of roasting duck and stewing cabbages, so sharply sweet with the fragrance of hot ginger and cinnamon from the bakery where Cream Puff Fatty fashioned his creations! A logger who was shaving would take a deep breath of this incense, and the blood would trickle unnoticed from a slash in his cheek; another, in his bunk would let his pipe slip from his hand and enjoy ardent inhalations, blissfully unaware of his burning shirt; yet another, engaged in greasing his boots, would halt his task and sit in motionless beatitude, his head thrown back, his eyes closed, quite unconscious of the grease that poured from a tilted can into a prized boot.

At half past eleven the hungriest of the loggers began to mass before the cookhouse door, and as the minutes passed the throng swiftly increased. At five minutes to noon all the bunkhouses were empty and the furthest fringe of the crowd was far up Onion River valley. The ground shook under a restless trampling, and the faces of the loggers were glowing and eager as they hearkened to the clatter and rumble inside the cookhouse, as four-horse teams hauled in loads of salt, pepper and sugar for the shakers and bowls. Then the loggers began to stamp and shout as they heard the flunkies, led by the Galloping Kid on his white horse, rushing the platters and bowls of food to the tables. Tantalizing smells wafted forth from the steaming dishes. The loggers grew more restless and eager; they surged to and fro in a tidal movement; jests and glad oaths made a joyous clamor over the throng. This was softened into a universal sigh as the doors swung open and Hot Biscuit Slim, in spotless cap and apron, appeared wearing the impressive

mien of a conquering general. He lifted an iron bar
with a majestic gesture, paused for dramatic effect
amid a breathless hush, and then struck a resounding
note from the steel triangle that hung from the wall.
At the sound a heaving torrent of men began to pour
through the doors in a rush that was like the roaring
plunge of water when the gate of a dam is lifted.
The chief cook continued to pound out clanging
rhythms until the last impatient logger was inside.

Then Hot Biscuit Slim reëntered the cookhouse.
He was reminded of a forested plain veiled in thin fog
as he surveyed the assemblage of darkly clad figures,
wreathed with white and fragrant blooms of steam.
His impression was made the more vivid when the
loggers plunged their spoons into the deep bowls of
oyster soup, for the ensuing sounds seemed like the
soughing of wind in the woods. The chief cook
marched to the kitchen with dignity and pride, glancing to right and left at the tables that held his master-
work. He asked for no praise or acclaim; the ecstasy
that now transfigured the plainest face was a sufficient
light of glory for him.

The soup bowls pushed aside, the loggers began to
fill their plates, which were of such circumference that
even a long-armed man could hardly reach across one.
The black ducks, of course, received first attention.
And great as the plates were, by the time one was
heaped with a brown fried drumstick, a ladle of duck
dumplings, several large fragments of duck fricassee,
a slab of duck baked gumbo style, a rich portion of
stewed duck, and a mound of crisp brown dressing, all

immersed in golden duck gravy, a formidable space was covered. Yet there was room for tender leaves of odorous cabbage beaded and streaked with creamy sauce; for mashed potatoes which seemed like fluffs of snow beside the darkness of duck and gravy; for brittle and savory potato cakes, marvelously right as to texture and thickness; for stewed tomatoes of a sultry ruddiness, pungent and ticklish with mysterious spices; for a hot cob of corn as long as a man's forearm, golden with sirupy kernels as big as buns; for fat and juicy baked beans, plump peas, sunny applesauce and buttered lettuce, not to mention various condiments. Squares of cornbread and hot biscuits were buttered and leaned against the plate; a pot-bellied coffee-pot was tilted over a gaping cup, into which it gushed an aromatic beverage of drowsy charm; a kingly pleasure was prepared. More than one logger swooned with delight this day when his plate was filled and, red-faced, hot-eyed, wet-lipped, he bent over it for the first mouthful with the joy of a lover claiming a first embrace.

In the kitchen the chief cook, the baker and their helpers watched and listened. At first the volume of sounds that filled the vast room was like the roar and crash of an avalanche, as dishes were rattled and banged about. Then the duck bones crackled like the limbs of falling trees. At last came a steady sound of eating, a sound of seventy threshing machines devouring bundles of wheat. It persisted far beyond the usual length of time, and Hot Biscuit Slim brought out his field glasses and surveyed the tables. The loggers were still bent tensely over their plates, and their elbows rose and fell with an energetic movement as they scooped up the food with undiminished vigor.

"Still eatin' duck," marveled Hot Biscuit Slim.

"They won't be more'n able to *smell* my cream puffs," said the baker enviously.

The loggers ate on. They had now spent twice their usual length of time at the table. Each plate was in a dark shadow from tall rows of slick black duck bones and heaps of corn cobs. But——

"Still eatin' duck," reported Hot Biscuit Slim.

That no one might see his grief Cream Puff Fatty moved to a dark corner. He was now certain that none of the loggers could have room for his pastries. They ate on. They had now spent three times their usual length of time at the table. The baker was sweating and weeping; he was soaked with despair. Then, suddenly:

"They're eatin' cream puffs!" cried Hot Biscuit Slim.

Cream Puff Fatty could not believe it, but a thrill of hope urged him to see for himself. True enough, the loggers were tackling the pastries at last. On each plate cream puffs the size of squashes lay in golden mounds. As the spoons struck them their creamy contents oozed forth from breaks and crevices. Stimulated by their rich flavor, the loggers ate on with renewed gusto. They had now stayed four times as long as usual at the table. Other enchantments still kept them in their seats: lemon pies with airy frostings, yellow pumpkin pies strewn with brown spice specks, cherry pies with cracks in their flaky crusts through which the red fruit winked, custard pies with russet freckles on their golden faces, fat apple pies all odorous with cinnamon, cool, snowy cream pies, peach cobblers, chocolate puddings, glittering cakes of many colors, slabs of gingerbread, sugar-powdered jelly rolls, doughnuts as large around as saucers and as thick through as cups, and so soft and toothsome that a morsel from one melted on the tongue like cream. So endearing were the flavors of these pastries that the loggers consumed them all.

Cream Puff Fatty and Hot Biscuit Slim solemnly shook hands. There was glory enough for both of them.

At last there were no sounds at the tables save those of heavy breathing. The loggers arose in a body and moved sluggishly and wordlessly from the cookhouse. They labored over the ground towards the bunkhouses as wearily as though they had just finished a day of deadening toil. Soon Onion River valley resounded with their snores and groans. . . .

At supper time, when Hot Biscuit Slim rang the gong, Cream Puff Fatty stood by his side. This was to be the supreme test of their achievement. For five minutes the chief cook beat the triangle, and then a solitary logger appeared in the door of a bunkhouse. He stared at them dully for a moment and then staggered back into the darkness. This was indeed a triumph! Great as other feasts in the cookhouse had been, never before had *all* the loggers been unable to appear for supper. This was a historic day. Cream

Puff Fatty and Hot Biscuit Slim embraced and mingled rapturous tears. It was their high moment. They would not have traded it for all the glory that was Greece and the grandeur that was Rome. . . . They had intimations of immortality. . . .

For five weeks the loggers lay in a delicious torpor, and then Johnny Inkslinger brought them from their bunks with doses of alcohol and Epsom salts. By this time the Big Swede had recovered from his injuries, and Paul Bunyan waited no longer to move his camp. The buildings, which rested on skids, were chained and cabled together, and the blue ox hauled them over the hills to the new job.

Nothing marred the beauty of that summer; stirring breezes blew all the days over the loggers as they felled the Leaning Pine trees in perfect lines on the grassy slopes. The blue ox waxed fat with the ease of his labor. Weeks passed without the Big Swede having a serious accident. Dust gathered on Johnny Inkslinger's medicine case. Hot Biscuit Slim never once failed to remember meat. And a record number of logs were piled above the rollways. Paul Bunyan planned a great drive with prideful confidence that it would be the glorious climax of a historic season. But here fortune deserted him, for, after driving the logs for nine days, and seeing an exact repetition of scenery three times, he had Johnny Inkslinger survey the placid river. The river was round; it flowed in a perfect circle; and Paul Bunyan had driven the logs three times over the same course!

Nothing daunted, he thereupon determined to saw

the logs and transport the lumber overland, and he
erected his famed sawmill, which was nineteen stories
high, with each bandsaw and each circular saw running
through all the floors.   A description of the original
machines and devices used in this mill would fill the
pages of a mail order catalogue.   It is needless to say
that it operated perfectly.   The only great difficulty
Paul Bunyan had to overcome originated from the
smokestacks.   He was compelled to equip them with
hinges and drawbridge machinery so that they could
be lowered to let the clouds go by.

THE OLD HOME CAMP

THE old home camp of Paul Bunyan, was in the Smiling River country; it lay in a great plain, between this sunny stream and the flowered banks of Honey Creek, which lazed on past the camp ere it joined the river. When the sun got low in the West, the shadow of old Rock Candy Mountain crept over the camp. On hot summer days the frost-hued mountain was a freshening sight; at night it looked like a huge dish of white ice cream. Raspberry trees covered its lower slopes, and in the Junetime they were heavy with berries as big as apples. The lemonade springs bubbled from among these trees, and their waters rippled through blossoming strawberry bushes as they coursed towards the river. In the twilights of the fruitful season the songs of the jaybirds that nested in the raspberry trees sank to a soft and sentimental chorus; and their slumbrous melodies, mingled with the cheery "jemine-e-es" of the jeminy crickets that lived among the strawberry bushes, made a beauty of sound harmonious with the spirit of eventide.

The old home camp had been built in the midst of a grove of maples. It had been deserted for seven years, and only a few moss-covered bunkhouses yet remained. Some bare sections of land, deeply corrugated, showed where the great cookhouse had stood; and trails that had been packed by the trampling of thousands of calked boots were still marked through lush growths of grass.

Paul Bunyan's farm was the source of his supplies; it was ruled by John Shears and worked by the scissor-bills. It covered the rich bottom lands below Honey Creek, and it extended for miles over the bordering hills. Huge red clover blooms tossed and nodded on crowns and slopes when the warm June breezes blew. When the two happy but sensitive bees, Bum and Bill, had got enough honey from them to fill the thirty-five hundred barrels which were required for the loggers' hot cakes each winter, John Shears and the scissor-bills mowed the hay and baled it. Then the milk cows were pastured on the stubble until winter-time. They did not have such grandiose names as are given to cows nowadays—no one in Paul Bunyan's time would have thought of naming a kind, honest heifer Wondrous Lena Victress or Dairylike Daffodil Sweetbread;—they were simply called Suke, Boss, Baldy and S'manthy, but they were queenly milkers. Boss was the great butter cow; John Shears had only to put salt in her milk, stir it a bit, let it stand for a while, and he would have tubfuls of the finest butter in the land. Suke's milk made wonderful bubbly hot cakes. Baldy's milk never soured, and it was especially good in cream gravy. S'manthy's milk was pretty poor stuff, but she had a vast hanker-ing for balsam boughs, and in the winter she would eat them until her milk became the most potent of cough medicines. It saved Paul Bunyan's loggers from many an attack of pneumonia. The grand flocks of poultry, which were ruled by Pat and Mike, the powerful and bellicose webfooted turkey gobblers, performed marvels of egg-laying and hatching. The snow hens, for example, would lay only in the winter-time; they made their nests in the snow and laid none but hard-boiled eggs. There were great vegetable gardens in the bottom lands; there the parsnips and carrots grew to such a depth that the scissor-bills had to use stump-pullers to get them out of the ground. It took two men an hour and a half to sever the average cabbage from its stalk. The potatoes grew to such a size that Paul Bunyan invented the steam shovel for John Shears to use in digging them out. In the chewing tobacco patch the tobacco grew on the plants in plugs, shreds and twists, and it was highly flavored by the natural licorice in the soil.

It would take pages to describe all of the marvels and splendors of Paul Bunyan's farm.

For five years now Paul Bunyan had not visited his farm or the old home camp. He himself knew nothing of farming; first and last he was a logger, so he had left his farm completely in the control of John Shears when the great move was made from the old home camp. He trusted without doubts his boss farmer, who was a powerfully religious man. Only his violent piety had made him a failure as a woods boss. The loggers could not *bear* to be preached to, and John Shears had insisted on preaching to them through every meal. But he managed the scissor-bills ably; they were men who had failed to make good as loggers and who had the calm and meek spirit of born farm hands.   John Shears had easily taught them to venerate him as a prophet, and they willingly worked sixteen hours a day for him, though the loggers had never worked more than twelve.

After Paul Bunyan's departure, John Shears had faithfully improved the farm, and at last it became so productive that even the endless freight teams of Shagline Bill could not move all its hay and produce to the far-away logging enterprises.   Then only the simple routine of farm work remained to be done, and this hardly fetched fourteen hours of labor a day from the scissor-bills, even in the harvesting season.   John Shears, always a terror for work, got dissatisfied.   He began to dream of strange, tempting projects of irrigation and land-clearing.   He let himself imagine Paul Bunyan's logging crews digging ditches, grubbing out stumps, and leveling hills into grand hay and grain fields.   Then his dream became an active idea.   If logging could somehow be prohibited, abolished, totally exterminated—what then?   The loggers would all have to turn farm hands, for farming would be the only remaining industry.   And then he, John Shears, the one and only master farmer, would become supreme over all of them; he would have Paul Bunyan's place, and the great logger would have to take a lesser rôle!   Soon, waking or sleeping, the idea was always in his mind.   It was the root of many plans, and at last it threw out a monstrous growth.   John Shears planned nothing else than to do away with Babe, the blue ox, who skidded all of Paul Bunyan's logs to the river landings, who was the mainspring, the central motive force, of all his logging operations. Logging without Babe could no more be imagined than rain without clouds. This plan was the source of the prodigious poison parsnip plot.

Parsnips were Babe's favorite delicacy, and John Shears was supposed to ship the parsnip crop to the logging camp each fall. But in the year in which the monstrous plot was hatched he did not dig the parsnips at all. He allowed them to go to seed instead, and now the parsnip patch was rank with a poisonous second growth. John Shears intended to dig them in another month and ship them to the camp. The blue ox would eat them and die, and then he, the boss farmer, should attain the power and triumph of his dreams.

Little Meery, the farm slavey, alone was kept in ignorance of John Shears' schemes, not because he was feared or distrusted, but because he seemed so lowly, abject and unimportant. He had scarcely more consequence in the farm life than one of the snow hens. He slept on a hard bunk under the kitchen sink. He was not allowed to associate with the scissor-bills. The only attention he ever received from them was when they made him the object of blows and ridicule. One time he had been Thomas O'Meery, the Irish Orphan, an aspiring young logger. The rich food served in Paul Bunyan's cookhouse had been his undoing. He became obese, rotund, unable to swing an ax. He got such heft and circumference that he was a nuisance. Whenever he fell down he would have to roll around until he could find a logger who would lift him to his feet. He was a danger also. One time he rolled down a hill and bounced head-on into a column of marching loggers. He flattened every one, and Johnny Inkslinger, the timekeeper and camp doctor, was busy all night setting their broken ribs. After this mishap, Paul Bunyan turned him over to John Shears. The boss farmer gave him the meanest job on the farm; he put him to washing the dishes and slopping the pigs. Little Meery finally became resigned to his grievous affliction and lowly lot, and a spirit of sublime meekness sustained him even when he was most cruelly treated.

This corpulent child of misfortune had a rare and charming soul. He alone, of all the toilers on the great farm, felt the pastoral loveliness of his surroundings. His day of toil done, he would part his hair, gather a bunch of clover blooms, take Porkums, his little lame pet pig under his arm, waddle over the footbridge that crossed Honey Creek, and in the grounds of the old home camp enjoy his one small pleasure in life. Sitting on an old maple log, he would pretend that he was a lean, muscular head faller in Paul Bunyan's camp and one of the great logger's favorites. He would see himself as a bunkhouse hero, walking in the shadows of the blue ox, living a grand, free life. What delight Little Meery had from such imaginings! What pity that they had to fade! Little Meery always tried to be bravely cheerful when the dream was done. He would force back his tears, return the comforting squeals of

Porkums with a trembling smile, then move gently among the jaybirds, which always gathered trustingly around his feet, and return to his cruel slavey's life with only thoughts of kindness and charity for John Shears and the scissor-bills. If Paul Bunyan could only have truly known that heart of gold!

One evening in the old home camp Little Meery's imaginings became more active than usual. He pretended that he was winning a felling championship, while Paul Bunyan applauded him. . . . He made great chips fly like buckshot, the loggers were a cheering host, he swung the ax violently at every stroke. . . . Too late he felt himself slipping from the maple log, and he rolled helplessly to the ground. As usual, he could not get back on his feet. He rolled to the footbridge, but he could not pass between the railings. He lay there until dawn, and no help came. The morning passed, and still he lay helpless. He was not found until John Shears came to the farmhouse for dinner and discovered the breakfast dishes unwashed.

"Did it on puppus, I bet!" roared the boss farmer. "I'd let ye lay there an' rot ef 'twarn't fer the dishes. I got a mind to whale ye anyhow, hi gravy!"

"Please, oh, please don't beat me, Mr. Shears," pleaded Little Meery. "I tried to roll home, honest I did."

The boss farmer brought an ellum club into view.

"Oh, *by* gosh! Mr. Shears——"

"Swearin', hey?"

"I meant to say 'my'—honest!"

"Didn't nuther. Ye used a 'by' word, an' ye know plagued well ye meant to be profane!"

"Oh! oh! oh!" screamed poor Little Meery, as the blows poured upon him. John Shears beat him until sundown, taking five minutes out of each hour for rest. . . . He raised the ellum club for a last terrific blow, and Little Meery bravely tried to stifle his sobs, as he waited to receive it. The cruel blow was never delivered. Two words stopped it.

"Here . . . John!"

The words seemed to be calmly spoken, yet the tones that made them filled the vast plain of the home camp and reverberated in thunderous echoes among all the hills. The trees shook, the surface of Smiling River broke into violent waves, the slopes of old Rock Candy were disturbed by the smoke and roar of an avalanche. John Shears quietly dropped his ellum club; Little Meery opened his eyes and saw near him a boot with a toe cap made of an elephant hide. Then he looked up and beheld the kindly bearded countenance of the good and mighty Paul Bunyan looming above him. Then John Shears hastily helped him to his feet and he limped between the boss farmer's ankles and out on the footbridge. There he stopped to look worshipfully on his hero, his lord, his king, Paul Bunyan, who shook hands solemnly with John Shears.

"I didn't expect ye to ketch me a frolickin' with one o' my men," said John Shears attempting a grin. "But I do like to frolic once in a while, jest like your loggers do."

"I'm glad that you have learned to play, John," said Paul Bunyan gently. "The playful spirit of my loggers has helped them to bear untold perils, griefs and hardships. They are a fine bunch of savages, worthy of emulation. I intend for them to enjoy the bounties and peace of home life for a season. We return to log off the rest of the Smiling River country."

"Well, now, I'm mighty glad you're to be with us again, Mr. Bunyan," said John Shears effusively.

"Thank you, John. And I wish to commend you for your faithful service. I hope to reward you fittingly. And I overlook your failure to ship Babe his parsnips last fall. Your one failure, for which I shall not reprove you. But you must prepare him acres of them at once. Understand? Very well. Yay, Babe!"

Johnny Inkslinger, the timekeeper, and the Big Swede, the foreman, were beside Paul Bunyan. The three moved towards the maple grove, and the blue ox, who had been straddling the river, stepped on across it, dragging the cookhouse, the bunkhouses, and the other camp buildings behind him. He was thin, and the shape of his great ribs showed through his shaggy blue hide. As he moved through the twilight shadows he looked like a wrinkled bluff when it is seen dimly in a fog. For half an hour the bunkhouses flashed by so swiftly that their lighted windows made an unbroken streak of light. The loggers in them were singing about the jam on Garry's Rock and the death of young Munro. As Little Meery listened to the roaring choruses he felt that he would willingly give

his life for a single day as a real logger.   If he could
only be there in one of the bunkhouses, a tough and
respected member of a logging crew, a lean, supple,
vigorous axman, a fine and admired figure!   Vain,
vain desire!   Poor Little Meery.   He abandoned the
dream with a sigh.   Then he was startled by a dry,
rasping chuckle from John Shears.   Little Meery was
astonished, for he had never heard the boss farmer
laugh.

"Parsnips, hey?" he cackled.   "Ol' Paul wants his
ox critter to have his parsnips right now, does he?
Dad gum', ef that ain't funny!   Ho! ho!"

The boss farmer leaped over Honey Creek and
strode rapidly towards the farmhouse.   Every hundred yards he would pause and chuckle convulsively.
"Parsnips, hey?   Ye dern' tootin' I'll feet him
parsnips!   It's Mr. Bunyan's pers'nal orders, says I.
Heh! heh!   Dad burn', ef that ain't funny!"

While Paul Bunyan, Johnny Inkslinger and the Big
Swede cruised the remaining timber in the Smiling
River country, the loggers renewed their affections for
the delights of the old home camp.   In the mornings
they roamed the cool slopes of old Rock Candy, they
gorged themselves with ripe fruit from the raspberry
trees and strawberry bushes, and, barefooted, they
climbed the maple trees and gamboled over the clover
fields.   In the afternoons Smiling River was splashed
with foam for miles as they swarmed into their old
swimming holes.   Swimming over, the loggers would
line up on the banks and shake their right legs to get
the water out of their left ears and their left legs to

get the water out of their right ears. Then they would angle for the bright-hued butterfish that fluttered among the water flowers. And what exhilarating meals they enjoyed! Now they had all the fresh stuff that the farm could provide. Cream Puff Fatty, the baker, made them strawberry shortcake and raspberry pie twice a day, and he covered these juicy confections with snowy piles of vanilla-flavored whipped cream. The cobs from golden, fat-kerneled roasting ears were soon heaped mountain-high in the kitchen yard. The cream gravy for the rosy new potatoes and bouncing green peas was made from real cream, sweet and thick. The loggers became light-hearted boys again, and as they enjoyed themselves they were happily unconscious of the bitter enviousness of the scissor-bills, who were digging parsnips for twenty hours a day on the other side of Honey Creek.

Babe, the blue ox, too, was enjoying life as never before. The stream from the lemonade springs had been diverted to a trough that ran through his manger; and he was surrounded with fresh, green clover, for John Shears, with sinister purpose, had mown all the clover fields on the day after Paul Bunyan's arrival and had stacked it in and around Babe's stable. He had hoped that the blue ox would bloat on the green feed, and perish before his master could return from his cruising expedition. But the early harvest had only served to throw the two bees into a rebellious rage; they had been imprisoned in their hive, and there, night and day, they had buzzed wrathfully over their half-filled honey barrels. Babe digested the green clover easily, and ate it with delight, his great blue eyes shining with affection and gratitude for the boss farmer.

"Pity 'tain't alfalfy, ye blame' hog," snarled John Shears in disgust.

But it wasn't, so John Shears made the scissor-bills work twenty hours a day in the parsnip patch, and he aided them with his own efforts, for he realized that once Paul Bunyan and Johnny Inkslinger had returned a fatal poisoning of the blue ox would be difficult to accomplish. He would not have the courage to attempt it then. Now was the time to strike. Heaven helping him, he should not fail!

During this week Little Meery had been kept within the bounds of the farmyard by the strict orders of John Shears. His heart was heavy indeed as he toiled away in the kitchen. Never had the scouring of pots and pans seemed to be such wretched labor; never had the odors and steam of dishwater seemed so detestable. When he went out to slop the pigs at eventide he heard the jaybirds' songs no more; he had ears only for the shouts, laughter and harmonies that sounded in the old home camp. Next week the grand life of logging would begin; all summer he, poor unfortunate, would suffer the misery of vain longings. Poor Little Meery; he looked in vain for a silver lining to his cloud.

Saturday came, and only one more holiday remained for the loggers to enjoy. As Little Meery listened to their exuberant noise, he was unable to drive away his despondency with songs or cheerful thoughts. Hour by hour his spirits got lower; his optimism left him, and his mind was dark with dismal shades. When he went to bed under the kitchen sink he did not fall into a sound sleep at once, as he usually did; his misery and dejection kept him awake. For two hours he lay there, soaking his pillow with tears, then the droning murmurs from the settin'-room were hushed, and, after a pause, John Shears began a speech. He fully revealed his frightful scheme to the scissor-bills, and he exhorted them to be true to his cause, which was their cause also. When Little Meery understood that the boss farmer intended to poison the blue ox and thus do away with the logging industry forever, he gave such a start of horror that his head banged against the bottom of the sink. The speech was halted at the sound.

"It's only Little Meery," said a scissor-bill contemptuously.

Little Meery did not venture to stir again as John Shears went on speaking.

"So it's all fixed to pizen the ox critter to-night," said John Shears in conclusion. "Then they'll be no more wicked loggin'. Loggin' must be wicked because it makes wicked men. Farmin' must be good because it makes good men. When ol' Paul Bunyan an' his loggers has to go farmin' they'll nacherlly turn into good men. Then they'll have to foller us, hi grabby, because we was farmers an' good men before they was. I hate to pizen a pore dumb critter, but this here's by way of makin' him a sackerfice—a sackerfice for the glory of life eternal! Glory! glory! glory!"

The scissor-bills all shouted "Glory! glory! glory!" after him, and then Little Meery heard them all move out of the settin'-room. For a few minutes he did not dare to stir, then he could no longer tolerate the anxiety of waiting. He slid carefully from his bunk, he took off his nightgown and slipped on his ragged slavey's clothes, and then, pausing cautiously at every heavy step, he approached the kitchen door. He opened it and peered outside. There was a fair light from a half-moon, and he could see the scissor-bills standing in rows and clusters along the barnyard fence. John Shears was already across Honey Creek. He opened the door of Babe's stable, and then ran back to the farmyard. Soon Babe's head appeared in the stable doorway, his great gentle eyes looked inquiringly about, then they shone hungrily as they glimpsed a white heap of the vegetables he loved. Other piles were scattered at intervals of seven hundred yards. In a short time Babe was in the parsnip patch, and he began to devour the first mountainous pile of the deadly vegetables. John Shears and the scissor-bills shouted halleluiahs of joy and triumph.

Horror, despair, a terrible sense of helplessness, held Little Meery motionless in the doorway. Hours seemed to pass as he frantically tried to think of some means to thwart the plot of John Shears and to ward off the tragic event that was swiftly casting its shadow over the old home camp. But what could *he* do? He was only Little Meery, scorned, despised, held in such contempt that he had been ignored entirely in the plans.

Then a sound that had roared in his ears ever since the clover was cut for the blue ox startled his mind with a desperate idea. The sound was the raging hum of two great bees, Bum and Bill, and Little Meery now resolved to release them from the hive, whatever the danger to himself. He knew that they would make a savage attack on the blue ox and perhaps drive him from the perilous parsnip patch. So he eased himself out of the kitchen and trod as softly as his obesity permitted towards the beehive. He reached it without being discovered, then he heaved up desperately on the latch. Up it went—six inches, twelve, eighteen, thirty-six, sixty—it was over the top of the block! As Little Meery pantingly threw the door open, the bees began to roar, then they shot out of the hive with a deafening buzz, their wings humming so violently that the wind from them stripped the shirt off his back. The bees zigzagged doubtfully for a moment, then they spied the blue ox in the parsnip patch. They cracked their wings together and lit out for him in a beeline. John Shears saw them and bawled for them to return, but, though they were obedient bees in their gentle moods, his yells now made them buzz on in a greater rage than ever. They circled the blue ox three times, then they sat on him and began a furious stinging of him. Babe bellowed. The scissor-bills were thrown through the barnyard fence when the wind from that bellow struck them, but John Shears charged through the vegetable gardens after the bees. And reached the anguished ox just as he had lifted his hind legs for a tremendous kick. Babe's hoof caught the boss farmer squarely between his eyebrows and his ankles, and he was hurled so high into the air that he sailed over the cloud-kissed crest of old Rock Candy. Babe flailed away mightily with his tail, he pawed up clouds of dirt, he stood on his horns, but the bees remained seated. At last the blue ox galloped out of the parsnip patch and ran for the sanctuary of his stable, where the bees dared not follow him.

Babe's bellow had rolled Little Meery among the scissor-bills, but he landed on his feet. He lumbered away from them in the direction of the footbridge, and when the scissor-bills had disentangled themselves from the splinters of the fence, they set out after him. They caught him in the center of the bridge, but just as they were beginning to beat him, the loggers, who had all been shaken from their bunks by Babe's anguished bellow, came with a rush from the other side. Then began the famous Battle of the Footbridge, in which the opposing forces vainly attempted to reach each other over the obese form of Little Meery, who received hundreds of blows a minute. All through the night the battle raged, while Babe mooed woefully in his stable and Bum and Bill buzzed gleeful satisfaction in their hive.

Not until sunrise, when Paul Bunyan reached the old home camp, was the terrible struggle ended. He ordered the loggers and the scissor-bills into the plain before the maple grove and demanded an explanation.

The combatants were too weary from their terrific struggle to reply, but at last Little Meery found strength to speak and told his awful story.

"Brave, brave heart," Paul Bunyan commended him. "And how can I reward you?"

"I want to be a head faller, Mr. Bunyan."

"But a head faller must fit into a head faller's uniform, and you my fine lad—well, you are Little Meery."

Then Little Meery staggered triumphantly from among the weary host. Not a stitch remained on him, he was bruised from head to heels, but he showed himself with pride. For he was not now the seven hundred and eighty pound Little Meery of yesterday, but a raw-boned two hundred and fifty pound logger, lean, solid and strong. During the long battle, pound by pound, over a quarter of a ton of fat had been pushed, prodded, punched, pounded, rolled, jerked, squeezed and stamped from his body. His obesity was gone! Miracle of miracles! Paul Bunyan could hardly believe his eyes.

"A head faller you shall be," he said.

John Shears was three weeks returning from the spot whither Babe had kicked him. Meek, humble, chastened, repentant, he came to Paul Bunyan and declared himself willing to submit to the dire punishment which he supposed awaited him. He expected to be made to eat gravel for a month, at the very least. The good and mighty Paul Bunyan, however, merely ordered John Shears to get back to the farm. But he put a ban on parsnips. As for Little Meery, when he heard that John Shears had returned, he twisted his hat around—his hair was never parted now,—he took a grand chew of fire cut, hitched up his tin pants and growled. "Let's walk on him! Let's put the calks to him! Let's cave his head in!" Little Meery had become a logger indeed, and he lived gloriously ever after.

SHANTY BOY

In Paul Bunyan's time, camp entertainment was of, by and for the woodsmen. In Paul Bunyan's camp there were hypnotic story-tellers, singers who could make you laugh and cry in the same moment, and steppers who could do a breakdown fit to shatter the frame of a bunkhouse. "Ol' Paul" knew the importance of social pleasures for his loggers, and he made natural provision for them. A good bunkhouse bard was marked by the great logger's especial favor; many a man who toiled poorly was saved from the lowly life of a farm hand by his ability to dance, whistle and sing. Consequently Paul Bunyan's Bunkhouse Nights are as famous in history as his great feasts and labors.

Every night but Sunday, when the twelve hours of toil in the woods were ended and supper was over, the tired loggers would be cheered and consoled by the bunkhouse bards. There was one for each shanty, and each one had his own particular virtues. There was Beeg An'tole, for example, who made his mates in Bunkhouse 999 hilarious as he told quaint tales about logging in "dat ver' fines' countree, which she's t'ree weeks below Quebec." Angus MacIlroy of Bunkhouse 1313 was made to sing "The Island Boys" a dozen times a night by his song-loving comrades.

And Tinty Hoolan of Bunkhouse 6000 jigged with such violence and speed that a modern jazz band would have gone crazy trying to make music fast enough for him. The rattle of his jigging feet sounded like the buzz of a big bee. His bunkhouse cronies boasted that he could imitate any known sound with his feet except a tired logger's snore. And this, anyone admitted, defied imitation or description. Tinty Hoolan was a swamper, and a poor one; his feet, however, saved him from life among the scissorbills on Paul Bunyan's farm.

Now these were three of the greatest of Paul Bunyan's bards, and no one has ever found words to describe them or to give them fitting praise. And if words fail with them, how can they reveal the brightest star of all Paul Bunyan's performers? Indeed, Shanty Boy, of Bunkhouse 1, was more than a star; he was a constellation, for he was an entertainer with a thousand talents. What old logger does not feel his own soul dance as he hears, in the Bunyan histories, the soft, vibrant patter of Shanty Boy's right foot, the thunderous stamp of his left foot, the sharp rattle of his heel-cracking in a great breakdown? He not only danced with his feet, but with his hands and eyes; he had a dancing grin, too, which would shine now on the right side of his face, now on the left. Shanty Boy put his whole soul into his dancing. And so he did with his stories. When he told a Swede story he *was* a Swede, and when he told a dirty story he *was* dirty. He was never content with mere pretending. He made entertainment of everything, and he did it naturally. A log would roll over his leg when he was at work. That night he would hobble down the bunkhouse aisle like an ailing old man, talking in the mournfullest way. "Oh, lawdy, boys! I 'low I ain't long fer *this* life. Thet new medicine I'm usin' don't 'pear to be doin' my rheumatiz no good, no good a-tall. I spect I'll be havin' to change to 'nuther kind agin." Then he'd hobble back again, drawing his sore leg up like a string-halted horse, and groaning, "M-m-m-! M-m-m! I 'low I feel worse'n anyone thet ever lived in this here world—an' lived." If somebody asked him what time it was, he would take out his old watch, hold it at arm's length, throw back his head and squint at the watch like he was looking at it through glasses. He claimed that "grandpap carried thet watch fer nigh on forty year, an' it won't tell the time onless I look at it jest like he did." Sometimes he would sit down by the stove and eat an apple or a raw turnip. Then he would pull his hat down over his eyes, and while he chewed away, looking as solemn as a politician, he would make the hat bob up and down to keep time with his jaws. No one else could have done this without seeming foolish, but Shanty Boy always kept a kind of dignity when he was performing that made men respect him even when they were laughing at him.

But it was his songs and stories which truly endeared him to the loggers. His renditions of "John Ross," "Jack Haggerty," "The Island Boys," and "Bung Yer Eye," were so affecting and inspiring that the loggers, what with laughing, crying, stamping, clapping and cheering, often made so much sympathetic noise that the song itself could not be heard. Shanty Boy only sang two nights a week and then for no longer than four hours at a time. The other nights he danced, and told true but thrilling stories of life in the woods. The bards from other bunkhouses would come to hear him and then give imitations of his performances. His supremacy was unquestioned, yet he remained unspoiled.

For he was more than a mere entertainer. The mightiest of Paul Bunyan's loggers lived in Bunkhouse 1, and as a logger Shanty Boy was the peer of any of them. He could notch a tree or work in white water with the best of the fallers and rivermen. He held his own with even Mark Beaucoup in the rough bunkhouse frolics. He was Paul Bunyan's favorite faller, and the great logger often carried him to the woods on his shoulder. He had an equal rank with Hot Biscuit Slim, the chief cook, Shagline Bill, the freighter, and Big Ole, the blacksmith. He was a true hero. And a time came when he reached the greatest height of glory ever attained by a plain logger. Here is how it came about.

The Year of the Two Winters had been disastrous for Paul Bunyan. Winter had come again in the summertime that year, and the cold increased in the succeeding months. At Christmas time there was fifty feet of ice on Lake Michigan, and by the last of February the lake was frozen to the bottom. Paul Bunyan was then engaged in logging off the Peninsula country, and of course his operations were halted. He cut the ice into blocks and hauled them out on the lake shore with Babe, his big blue ox, who could pull anything that had two ends on it. This was done so that the ice would melt more quickly when normal summer weather returned. Then he moved his outfit to the old home camp in the Smiling River country, where severe weather was never experienced.

Paul Bunyan had done no logging around his old home camp for seven years. The remaining timber was so far from the river and on such steep hills that profitable logging seemed impossible. However, it was the best to be had, for elsewhere it would be weeks, even months, before the snow drifts would melt away from the tree tops. Paul Bunyan tackled the tough logging problems before him with characteristic courage. He was sure that his inventiveness and resourcefulness would, as always, triumph over every obstacle.

His most stubborn and difficult problem was that of getting the loggers to the woods in the morning in time to do any work and getting them home at night in time to do any sleep. One plan after another was tried and dropped, failures all. Paul Bunyan began with an attempt to work one day shift, but the loggers could not get to the woods before lunch time; lunch finished, they had to start at once for the camp. Two shifts were then put on, but little work could be done at night, except when the moon was full. Paul Bunyan then sent the great Johnny Inkslinger, his timekeeper and man of science, to investigate the

Aurora Borealis as a means of artificial lighting.
Johnny reported that it was pretty but unreliable, and
he doubted if even the blue ox could move it down
from the North in less than six months. The learned
Inkslinger then sat down and figured desperately for
a week, trying to devise a method of working three
twelve-hour shifts a day. With such a routine one
shift could be doing a day's work, while a second shift
was coming to work, and a third was going to camp.
Johnny Inkslinger was, beyond a doubt, the greatest
man with figures that ever lived, but here his math-
ematics failed him. Paul Bunyan then thought of
making a campsite in the timber, and he dug for water
in the high hills. He succeeded in reaching a mighty
vein, but it was so deep that it took a week to draw a
bucket of water out of the well. It was out of the
question as a water supply for the camp.

Now Paul Bunyan had to fall back on a last plan,
a far-fetched one that seemed well-nigh hopeless.
This was to build a great sled, something on the order
of a lunch sled, and have Babe, the blue ox, haul the
loggers to and from work each day. It was a desperate plan, and no one but Paul Bunyan would have
had the courage to attempt it. It must be remembered
that the blue ox measured forty-two ax handles and a
plug of chewing tobacco between the horns; an
ordinary man at his front had to use a telescope to see
what he was doing with his hind legs, he was so long;
he had so much energy and such delight in labor that
no one could hold him when he started for the woods in
the mornings; he was so fast that Paul Bunyan's fore-

man, the Big Swede, who was as tall as the trees, could not begin to keep up with him. Only Paul Bunyan could travel so fast.   Whenever Babe moved the camp he traveled at a careful pace, but even then some of the loggers were made seasick; and all of them became so irritable when a move was being made that they fought constantly among themselves.   If the comparatively slow camp-moving pace of the blue ox thus upset them, his timber-going gallop would be apt to ruin them completely.   Paul Bunyan remembered how the Big Swede, hanging to Babe's halter rope, was hurled through the air, only striking the ground once in every quarter of a mile or so, when the blue ox rushed to his delightful labor each morning.   A lunch sled full of loggers would be dragged by Babe in much the same fashion; it would be in the air most of the time, and when it did strike the ground loggers would be scattered like autumn leaves.   The loggers who would hang on until the woods were reached would have the living daylights shaken out of them.   A common lunch sled would not do; one must be invented that would hold the road.

So Paul Bunyan devised the serpentine bobsled. It was a long, low-built contraption; the runners were made in short sections, connected by double joints. When it was completed and lay in the road that led from the camp it looked like a squat fence, for it snugly fitted the contours of the hills and vales over which it extended.

"There's a rig that'll hold the road," said Paul

Bunyan with pride. "Now I'll invent something equally good to hold Babe to a slow pace."

Several mechanical devices were tried without passing the first test. The sled lay idle. The loggers got sore feet, and they traveled so slowly that they began to take twelve hours to reach the woods. There was one shift on the road, going, and one coming all of the time. Not a tree was being felled.

"There's no way out of it but to try the grizzlies," Paul Bunyan told his timekeeper.

Among the other livestock on Paul Bunyan's farm, which was down the river from the old home camp, was a herd of grizzly bears. The great logger often amused himself by playing with them, and he had taught them many tricks. Not the least of their stunts was for each bear to hang from a tree with three paws and try to claw Paul Bunyan's mackinaw with the other paw as he dodged by.

"I'll station them at the trees which are left standing along the road," said Paul Bunyan, "and when Babe roars by they'll hook him. They may only frighten him into a faster run, but I think surely they'll slow him down."

The next morning the loggers, for the most part, joyfully crawled upon the serpentine bobsled. The timid and cranky among the loggers were pessimistic, of course, and declared noisily that this would be the end of them. But Shanty Boy and the other bards laughed at their fears, and at last every logger in camp was on the sled. Paul Bunyan ordered the Big

Swede to hitch up the blue ox and start in half an hour, and he departed for the woods with his herd of grizzlies. He stationed one of them at every tree close to the road. When he reached the timber he straddled a hogback and sat down to wait for the outcome of his daring attempt.

In a short time he heard a faint thunder down in the valley, then he saw enormous balloons of dust twisting up in cyclonic bursts from the foothills, next he heard the crashing sound of hoofbeats that got louder and louder. . . . Through clouds of dust he saw Babe's tail brush lifted like a triumphal banner and the glitter of his horns. . . . The Big Swede, hanging to Babe's halter rope, soared and dived. . . .

The bears had failed. Indeed, they had failed terribly, for when Babe came to a halt in the timber Paul Bunyan saw bears paws hanging from both sides of him. Only one bear had saved his paw, and he was holding a tree in a frenzied clutch. Babe had carried away bear, tree and all. Paul Bunyan rushed back over the road, and as he came to each unfortunate grizzly he mercifully dispatched him. He carried them all into camp.

"Bear meat for Sunday dinner," he said to Hot Biscuit Slim, as he threw the bears into the kitchen yard.

Paul Bunyan then had Johnny Inkslinger bring his medicine case, and the two hurried to the woods. But only a slight number of the loggers had been made truly ill by the terrific speed with which Babe had hauled them over the hills. The double-jointed sled runners had slipped over rocks, logs and gullies as easily as a snake glides over a string. Not once had the sled bounded from the road. Not a logger had suffered a jolt. Some of them were dazed and breathless, others were choked with dust, but most of them were no more than badly scared by their terrific journey.

"Aye tal you it ban no use try hol' Babe down," said the Big Swede, with rare eloquence.

"The sled worked perfectly, at any rate," said Paul Bunyan. "We can depend on it. But those good bullies of mine are going to need a lot of encouragement to stand that ride every morning."

He was quite right. His loggers thought nothing of the perils of falling limbs, which are called "widow-makers" to-day in the woods. Breaking up log jams, jumping rolling logs, dodging butts of trees which bucked back from the stumps when they fell—all this was in the day's work. But even the serpentine bobsled could not banish the terrors of riding behind the blue ox each morning. "I'd ruther try ridin' a peavy handle down the West Branch." "I'll tell you Babe went so fast I acshuly *seen* the wind, an' I never seen anything more sickenin' in my life!" "What if Babe ud a throwed a shoe now? I bet it 'da tore through us like a cannon ball!"

Paul Bunyan frowned as he hearkened to their complaints. His loggers seldom thought of anything but their labor when they were in the woods. If they were complaining now, what would happen when the bunkhouse cranks got into action after supper? There would be much gloomy grumbling, and perhaps rebellious talk. When the loggers went to bed they would brood over the cyclonic morning ride instead of getting fortifying sleep. Then they would soon balk against riding behind the blue ox. To avoid such an event he must call on his bards to cajole, humor and inspire the men until he could devise new methods to solve his logging problems. With this idea in mind he took Shanty Boy aside, placed him on his knee and explained the situation.

"I shore will do my best," said Shanty Boy. "But looky here, Mr. Bunyan, I 'low I'll have to lie to 'em right smart."

"How so, my lad?"

"Well I've allus done the best I knowed how when I set out to be amusin'. So, if I'm goin' to make my stories any thicker, I'll jest about have to stir a few lies into 'em."

"Son, nobody loves a liar."

"Thet's jest it, Mr. Bunyan. I got a powerful good reppytation fer truth, an' I can lie quite a spell afore I'm ketched. But if I do get ketched Mark Beaucoup an' them Rories'll chaw me up. You've learnt all the loggers to hate lyin' jest like you do yourself. I'd probably get spiled if I was ketched. Besides, I jest nacherly hate to lie. Yet, no lyin', no loggin', seems to be the fact o' the matter."

Paul Bunyan pondered doubtfully for some time. Moral issues baffled him always. But at last he spoke with decision.

"Logging must go on. You may lie, if necessary, during the period of emergency."

"Them's orders, Mr. Bunyan. But what if the gang gets hostile an' starts to chaw me up?"

Again Paul Bunyan hesitated. It was against his policy to interfere in the logger's personal affairs. Then, firmly:

"A man with your talent should not have to lie, Shanty Boy, in order to entertain his mates. But you know best, of course. If you are discovered, tell the men that all complaints must be lodged with me before they act upon them. Be cautious and discreet, and honor and glory shall be yours."

"I will, sir. Thank ye, sir, Mr. Bunyan."

Shanty Boy went bravely to work carrying out the great logger's commands. For some time it was not necessary to tell more than two or three lies a week in order to take the logger's thoughts off their sickening morning rides. They were not great lies that he told, either, but only plausible exaggerations. Most of his stories were still true ones, and he told them better than ever. He inspired the visiting bards as never before. Each night he sent his mates smilingly to sleep, entirely forgetful of the ordeal that awaited them in the morning. But this was not natural, and of course it couldn't last. The loggers lost weight every day, and they began to complain of hurts in their innards. The bunkhouse cranks got their dismal chorus started, and Shanty Boy had to tell real big lies to hush it.

He lied wonderfully indeed, once he was well started. He got so funny that the loggers had to strap themselves into their bunks while they listened to him. They went to sleep laughing, as a rule, and the night long they would chuckle in their dreams.

Shanty Boy grew bolder with success. He told, with a bare face, stories about snakes that had many joints, and how they would separate into pieces and crawl a dozen ways at once. He called them joint snakes. He told stories about a snake that would put its tail in its mouth and roll down hill. He called it a hoop snake. When the loggers got a little tired of snakes, he told whoppers about possums, then about coons, and so on. At last he got around to fish, and he told so many good fish stories that the loggers would not let him switch to another subject. He ran out of ideas, but the loggers would not let him get away from fish.

One night as he was trying desperately to invent a tolerable lie about fish he remembered a story of a whale that he had heard his grandfather tell, insisting that it was the gospel truth. It was the old story about Jonah and the whale, and the loggers had never heard it. They became indignant when Shanty Boy repeated it for the plain truth, and some of them began to shout at him. For the first time in his life he got stage fright. He felt that he was telling the gospel truth, but the memory of his previous lies overwhelmed him. He tried vainly to continue his narrative about Jonah's life in the whale's belly, but his tongue failed. He dropped his head, and he

fixed a shamed gaze on his feet. First he heard
nothing but the pounding of his heart; then an angry
mutter ran along the bunks. It grew into a fierce
growl. Then Shanty Boy heard the tramp of feet,
and he looked up to see Mark Beaucoup and the
bunkhouse cranks advancing upon him.

"She's lie!" yelled Mark Beaucoup. "*Sacre!* but
she's tell a beeg wan."

He shook a huge brown fist under Shanty Boy's nose.

"Now you are feex yourself. Stan' up w'ile I
knock you down!"

The loggers left their bunks and made a pressing
crowd around their discomfited bard and his chal-
lenger.

"I was coun' for you stan' up. Wan—two—
t'ree——"

Then Shanty Boy remembered Paul Bunyan's "All
complaints must be lodged with me" and courage
returned to him.

"You bunkhouse cranks shore give me a misery,"
he said contemptuously. "You jest go an' tell my
story to ol' Paul an' see what *he* says about it."

The loggers stared at him with amazement.

"By gar!" exclaimed Mark Beaucoup. "De fool
wan' me tell dees to ol' Paul! She's wan' me tell
dees, dat crazy t'ing!"

"Thet's what I said," growled Shanty Boy. "Run
along afore I get into one o' my tantrums."

Knowing Paul Bunyan's furious opinion of liars, the
loggers were smitten with horror. Of course this
story might not be a lie, but most likely it was, and

what old Paul would do to him for telling it! Mark Beaucoup was triumphant. Soon Bunkhouse 1 would have another king; it should know a rule of iron instead of laughter.

"Come wit' me," he commanded his friends. The other loggers, except Shanty Boy, followed them to Paul Bunyan.

As Paul Bunyan listened to Mark Beaucoup he was struck with a powerful regret for having inspired his greatest bard to leave the path of truthful narration. Desperate circumstances had seemed to justify the step. But what a risk he had taken just to save a few weeks logging! The faith his loggers had in him lay in the balance. Now it seemed that he must lose this faith or sacrifice a hero. He had never dreamed that Shanty Boy would recklessly tell such an incredible story. Surely he had not told it unthinkingly. No doubt he could explain it. Paul Bunyan sent for him.

It was with a heavy heart that the great bard walked through the lines of silent, accusing loggers. It looked like the end of everything for him. But he kept his courage, and, as he walked slowly on, his nimble mind was leaping from idea to idea, seeking a solid defense. But what proof could he offer for such a story? His grandfather *knew* it was true, but the old man was far away in the Southern mountains. He alone must prove somehow that he had not lied. . . . Paul Bunyan's boots loomed before him. . . . He must think hard . . . hard. . . .

"This story must be *explained*," said Paul Bunyan

in a stern voice, at the same time flashing him a look of the utmost sympathy.

"I 'low the story is beyond explainin', Mr. Bunyan, but I never lied when I told it," said Shanty Boy, bravely.

"Prove it!" roared Mark Beaucoup and his followers.

Shanty Boy drew himself up pridefully and he fixed upon the multitude a gaze of lofty scorn.

"I never lied!" he declared. "I never lied, for when I lie my neck *it swells!* An'—now—look!"

He jerked open the collar of his shirt and exposed his muscular throat. There was not a sign of swelling about it. The loggers lifted a mighty cheer, and Mark Beaucoup, baffled, beaten, completely outwitted, could only swear:

"She's don' swell—by gar!—she's don' swell!"

Paul Bunyan could not restrain a windy sigh of relief. The trees bent before the blast and dust clouds rolled through the ranks of loggers. Now was the moment to complete the victory.

"Get to your bunkhouses!" Paul Bunyan roared.

Shanty Boy was carried on the shoulders of yelling admirers to Bunkhouse 1. Mark Beaucoup and the bunkhouse cranks did not venture to follow them until the lights had gone out. Then, humbled and quiet, they sneaked into their bunks.

As a result of his troubles Paul Bunyan came near to abandoning logging operations in the Smiling River Country. But one night he got an idea, an idea so simple and sound that he was astonished at not think-

ing of it before.   He put it into practice at once, and
when the loggers awoke the next morning they saw
wooded hills at the very door of the camp.   Paul
Bunyan had simply thrown a cable around each hill,
and the blue ox, who could pull anything that had a
top on it, had snaked every one into camp.   So the
logging then went on easily until the new summer had
melted the ice and snow and Lake Michigan was filled
with water once more, and had new fish in it.

Shanty Boy's triumph was complete.   Not only did
he have great honors from Paul Bunyan, but his mates
now revered as well as admired him.   His ventures
from truth had held off revolt from the bunkhouses.
He had convinced the loggers of the truth of the grand
old story of Jonah and the whale.   And he had made
them all fear swelled necks as the result of lying.
This last effect persists to this day, for everywhere
loggers are still known as the most truthful of men.

THE KINGDOM OF KANSAS

No region of Real America, save Kansas, boasted of its weather in Paul Bunyan's time. In the heyday of the mighty logger the climates and seasons were not systematized; they came and went and behaved without rule or reason. There were many years with two winters, and sometimes all four seasons would come and go in one month. The wind would frequently blow straight up and then straight down. Sometimes it would simply stand still and blow in one place. In its most prankish moods it would blow all ways at once. The weather was indeed powerful strange in those days and it got itself talked about. And nowhere were its ways more evil than in Utah.

When Paul Bunyan moved his camp to the state of Utah for the purpose of logging off its forests of stonewood trees he was not careless of the climate; he merely failed to suspect its treachery. Besides, other troubles beset him. The gritty texture of the stonewood timber dulled the edge of an ax bit in two strokes. At the end of their twelve-hour day in the woods the loggers had to sharpen axes for seven hours. They were always fagged out. Then there was only one small river near the forests, and Babe, the blue ox, who had got hayfever again since coming West, drank it dry every fifteen minutes. The loggers thirsted, and they were bedeviled by sand in their blankets and in the beans, for every time Babe sneezed he raised a dust storm that rolled its clouds through the cookhouse and the bunkhouses and covered the great plain and the hills around the camp. A spirit of dark and evil melancholy settled on the loggers.

Paul Bunyan hoped for an adequate water supply from the December snows. And he brought all his inventive powers to the problem of felling the stone-wood trees. In eleven days and nights he devised eight hundred and five systems, machines and implements, and from this galaxy he selected a noble tool.

Paul Bunyan's new invention was the double-bitted ax, which is used everywhere in the woods to-day. Paul Bunyan devised it so that a faller could chop with one blade, then twist the handle and whet the other blade on the gritty stonewood with the backward swing.

But even with the new axes the logging went on slowly. The camp supply of elbow grease gave out, and the loggers suffered stiffened joints. The December snows were light, and the thirsty blue ox continued to drink the entire water supply. The bunkhouses came to be dens of ominous brooding and quiet instead of gay and noisy habitations. Finally the shipment of webfooted turkeys from the Great Lakes arrived too late for Christmas dinner. The loggers became dour, gaunt, embittered men.

Then came New Year's Day and outrageous fortune. When the loggers went to work at the first thinning of darkness they attributed the peculiar oppressive warmth of the morning to an unusual Chinook wind. There was, however, no wind at all. . Then the rising sun shot blazing rays into a cloudless sky. Even then the loggers did not realize that they were witnessing an Event. This was the beginning of a notable year, the Year of the Hot Winter. As the sun climbed higher the heat grew more intense. The Christmas snow had vanished at the first burning touch of day. The ground baked and cracked. The stonewood trees glittered in a fierce light. Each logger threw off his mackinaw, muffler, sweater, stagged shirt, woolen overshirt and undershirt, his parrafin pants, mackinaw pants and overalls and his Arctic socks, heavy wool socks, light wool socks and cotton socks. All heavy clothing was speedily thrown aside, and everywhere in the plain, in the valleys, and on the hillsides were piles of garments, and by each pile a logger toiled, clad only in drawers and calked boots. But still sweat dripped and trickled from their bodies; they labored more and more languorously. Each quarter of an hour the blue ox, with lolling tongue, dashed madly for the river and drank it dry.

Paul Bunyan was distressed by this change in his affairs, but he was not daunted. Confident that his loggers would do their best in the meanwhile, he again retired to solitude, hoping to devise something that would conquer the hostile and unnatural season. He returned with the great timber scythe, with which he could fell a full section of timber with one swing of his mighty arms. Carrying the timber scythe over his shoulder, Paul Bunyan strode toward his camp.

His tread was vigorous despite the deadening heat. Benevolent ideas stirred his heart. He himself would do the arduous labor of felling the stonewood trees; the loggers would be asked only to do the lighter work of trimming and bucking the trees into logs. They were a fine bunch of savages; ordinarily they would not allow even Paul Bunyan to do their natural work. Perhaps they would resist such intrusion now. But the great logger was sure of his persuasive powers.

As he neared the camp, busy as he was with philanthropic thoughts, he failed to note an unusual silence in the woods and about the bunkhouses. Not until he saw Babe and the Big Swede sleeping in the stable was he made aware of the extraordinary. Paul Bunyan went next to the camp office. Johnny Inkslinger, that tower of energy, was sleeping at his desk! His fountain pen had dropped from his hand, and as it was fed by hose lines from tweny-five barrels of ink, a black stream gushed from its point and flooded the floor. A chorus of faint snores came from each bunkhouse. The cookhouse looked gloomy and deserted. In the woods the axes and saws lay where the loggers had left them. For one hundred and seventy-nine minutes Paul Bunyan stood silently in the midst of his camp, tormented by wrath, regret and sorrow. His outfit had failed him. After all these years of comradeship in labor they had allowed a mere hot winter to provoke them into faithlessness. He had left them without an idea that they would be untrue to the job while he was scheming to make it a success.

But they had weakened. Very well, he thought, after his brief period of emotion, he would perform their labor for them while they snored. They should awaken to shame.

One stride brought him into the first clearing made among the stonewood trees. Without losing a second, he threw the timber scythe from his shoulder, he grasped its handles, then took a long swing, and the first section of trees thundered to the ground. On he went, making a circular swath. As he stepped with his right foot the sharp scythe blade crashed through the trees on the cutting stroke, and as he stepped with his left he brought the scythe behind him with a vigorous swing. On and on he labored, his steps coming faster as the circle widened. Every seven hours he paused to whet the blade of the timber scythe on a bundle of the stonewood trees which he carried in his hip pocket. The hot winter drove its fires upon him, but his passion of toil repelled them with a stronger flame. The great logger's walk became a run; the dazzling blade of the timber scythe flashed in strokes of inconceivable rapidity; the sections of stonewood trees fell in a steady roar.

Then Paul Bunyan began to sweat. He had labored before this, but never so savagely, nor in such penetrating heat. Only the man who raises a good sweat for the first time can realize what an astounding store of perspiration the human body can hold. On occasion it gushes from innumerable springs, seeming inexhaustible. It streams down the crevices and valleys of the body and floods the flat spaces; it soaks the clothing and drips to the ground. Imagine then what happened when Paul Bunyan's stored perspiration was unloosed. As he toiled on, ever more fiercely, his sweat flooded his boots, it surged over their tops and foamed towards the ground like two Niagaras. His swinging body and flying arms flung out clouds of spray. These strange waters coursed over the plains in torrents and gathered in heaving pools. The little river was submerged, drowned, exterminated. The waters crept towards the camp. Paul Bunyan, more and more engrossed with his labor as time went on, did not note the rising flood. His circle grew wider and wider. It left the plain and swung around the bordering slopes. Section after section of the trees was felled, only to be covered by water, for the stonewood timber was too heavy to float. But Paul Bunyan labored around and around the circle, quite unaware of the tragical consequence of his efforts.

For five days and nights the loggers lay in their bunks, too lazy to get up to eat, too lazy to do aught but drowse and dream. But at twelve o'clock on the fifth night the waters had reached the bunkhouses, and they learned of their peril. Yells of fear arose from every quarter, and in a few moments the whole camp, with the exception of Babe, the Big Swede, and Johnny Inkslinger, was aroused. Fright made the loggers forget the hot winter, and gave them energy. When they looked out on a vast lake glittering in the moonlight, and saw in the dim distance the twin rivers roaring from Paul Bunyan's boots, they knew that speedy and efficient action was necessary to save their lives. The best swimmers swam out to the tool house and brought back hammers, saws and nails. Each logger then began to build a boat from his bunk, and for three hours they worked feverishly and silently constructing the vessels. When the last one was finished the word was passed along and in a few moments the boats, each one carrying a logger and his blankets, swarmed from the bunkhouses. Before the armada had gone twenty feet the boats all filled with water and sank, while the loggers uttered lamentable cries. These changed to sounds of rejoicing, however, when it was discovered that the water was only waist deep. The loggers rescued their bundles from the boats and scampered to the shore like a holiday host at a beach.

But their joy did not last; it quickly gave way to dread. Paul Bunyan, toiling more desperately every moment, was rapidly moving around the circle. In a short time he would be upon them, and at any instant he might discover the fate of his trees, the flooding of his camp, his complete disaster. The loggers all understood the reason for the mighty man's wrathful labor. Their sense of blame confused them and smothered their native courage. The host began to move over the hills, haltingly at first, and with heads bowed like penitents. Then, as the volleying thunder of Paul Bunyan's timber scythe sounded nearer and nearer, they lifted their heads and struck a faster pace. Then guilty fears possessed them and every logger of the lot began to gallop madly. Someone yelled, "Ol'

Paul's a comin'!" and the warning cry was echoed from thousands of throats all over the hills. The loggers were taken by panic; the runaway became a stampede. By dawn they were making such running leaps that each logger would hit his chin with his front knee and his head with his back heel at every stride. They were so scared that they never stopped until they got to Kansas.

Now Kansas at that time had the only kingdom that was ever known to exist in this country. The ruler of Kansas was King Bourbon, and Topeka was his capital. The Kansas country was then one of the pleasantest in Real America. It was rolling land, like that everywhere else, but its heavy vegetation and its forests were beautiful and unique, and the climate and seasons were always spring; and indeed the history of Paul Bunyan's time tells of a year in Kansas that had thirteen months of spring.

The forests were mostly whisky trees, which grew amid carpets of cigarette grass and were entwined with beervines. The greatest of these forests was around Lake Topeka, and by the lake was the capital city, where the nobility and gentry of Kansas led a pleasurable life and envied no one.

When Paul Bunyan's loggers reached Kansas they were so exhausted from their long run that they had no eyes for the beauties of that region; they only felt that it invited them to rest and promised them security. So when they came to the banks of Rolling River they dropped on the soft and fragrant masses of cigarette grass, and rested in the cool shade of the spreading whisky trees, with the bliss known only to the utterly weary. For a long while they were not aware of the virile odors of the beervine blossoms, and they heard but faintly the melodies of the huge but gentle piano birds who were everywhere in the forest, either flitting from bough to bough or sitting in their nests. And even when they were rested and soothed by the sweet airs and tinkling melodies the loggers enjoyed the originality of their environment but a short while, for each one became conscious of a raging hunger.

"Let's look for a nose bag!" the cry up and down the columns and lines. The loggers all arose with the intent of foraging in the forest, and they would no doubt have appeased their hunger at once, if an impulsive curiousity had not made them take a last look at the river. A great gasp of astonishment went up, then a terrific crash of laughter shook the vast forest and silenced the piano birds. The loggers, one and all, dropped again to the ground and rolled and bounced about in convulsions of merriment.

Rolling River was a stubborn and valiant stream, and, unlike tamer rivers, it refused to follow the easiest course. From its source extended a range of hills which decreased in height until it was merged in the slope of a far valley. Rolling River made its way up and down these hills, cleaving each summit. At the place where the loggers were resting the river always had a hard fight, as one hill was nearly equal in height to the one that preceded it. Sometimes Rolling River would fail here; the waters would part at the summit, and one end of the river would go rushing on and the other end would slide back down the hill for a fresh start.

It was then that the giddyfish which dwelt in this stream would perform so clownishly as to tickle any observer into fits. Bewildered by the waters' abrupt desertion of them, and perplexed as to which end of the river it was best to follow, numbers of them would hesitate on the hilltop, agitated and floundering, then half of them would take out after the lower end of the river and half of them would take out after the upper end. They could make great speed by leaping along like kangaroos, using their long fins and tails. But they traveled clumsily, and their limber tongues lolled from their mouths as they leaped down the hillside, all of which made their every action seem inexpressibly humorous.

There was never an army of men who enjoyed a good laugh more than Paul Bunyan's loggers. And when they saw the giddyfish galloping after the river they laughed till they cried. When the river finally made it up the hill and began to roll on as usual the loggers could hardly stop laughing even then. But they remembered their hunger, and they again got up to search for food. But no sooner had they started than the river parted again, and once more the loggers rolled and laughed over the performance of the giddyfish. And indeed for fifty-seven hours the loggers were unable to get away from the riverside, for no sooner would they start to leave than the stubborn river and the clownish giddyfish would repeat their hilarious performance. The loggers would no doubt have laughed themselves to death, or else starved, had not King Bourbon come along with his race horses and jockeys and saved them.

King Bourbon had his jockeys make a wall of horse-flesh between the laughing loggers and the river, and they were then able to stagger back into the safety of the forest. The king then made the loggers a speech of apology and warning. He told them that the only crimes punishable by death in Kansas were dealing from the bottom of the deck, throwing a horse race or a fight, and shooting craps with loaded dice. Those convicted of such crimes were sentenced to watch the giddyfish until they laughed themselves to death. The king then asked the loggers at what games and contests did they excel, and when they told him of their expertness at spinning logs in rough water his face shone with a joy that made it brighter than the diamond in his necktie; for this new sport promised to be a thrilling one. He ordered his lord bookmaker to bring them on to the capital and find a place for them in the life of the city. After giving this order, he courteously lifted his plug hat to the loggers and, followed by his jockeys, he set out for Topeka, which was over the next hump.

After three days the loggers were themselves again and they began to explore the delights of the city.

Topeka, under King Bourbon's rule, was a city of amusements. There were eleven racetracks, and on each one there were seven races every afternoon. Each morning there were five baseball games, the first one beginning at four A. M. Boxing and wrestling matches, swimming and running races, driving and jumping contests were to be seen each Sunday in the stadium which faced Lake Topeka. In the time between races and contests the people played poker, solo, rummy and pool, and shot craps in the palace, which was the one public building in the city. In its single vast room there were countless tables for the players, and these tables were circled by a bar of such circumference that a man would grow a beard while walking the length of it. The glitter of the glasses and mirrors back of the bar was so brilliant and the jackets of the bartenders were so white that a beholder seemed to look on ice and snow which dazzlingly reflected sunlight. But the eye was soothed indeed when its gaze dropped to the dusky mahogany bar and searched the amber depths of a huge glass which frothed with the sharp and fragrant liquid brewed from foamy beervine blossoms. Even more was the eye delighted when it caught the jolly winks that bubbled from the most potent and jovial beverage, the aged sap of the whisky tree. One part of the bar was a great free lunch counter, which was always loaded with filling and peppery food. Here the nobility and gentry of Topeka ate and drank, King Bourbon, his lord bookmaker and his lord bartender among all the rest. The cooks, waiters and dishwashers had been working three shifts on the free lunch counter, but King Bourbon generously offered Paul Bunyan's kitchen crew employment there, and the lord bartender then had to divide the day into forty-eight shifts in order to have work for everyone.

The loggers were royally received into the grand life of Topeka. The skill they displayed in spinning logs on the lake each Sunday won them an honored place in the kingdom. They became tireless players of poker, solo, rummy, craps, and even of pool. They drank huge quantities of beervine brew and whisky tree sap. The free lunch made them forget the delights of Paul Bunyan's dinners. Soon they ceased to consider themselves as working loggers, and they repelled with scorn proposals to try a new life of toil, which were slyly made by followers of Duke Dryface, who was a cousin of the King.

The duke was secretly planning a revolt. He had renounced Topeka life, and he now lived among the serfs who brewed the beervine blossoms, aged the sap of the whisky trees, and made all of the materials that composed the grand life of Topeka. The serfs were called Cornmen, after a harsh cereal which they had devised, and which they all raised in clearings among the whisky tree forests. Duke Dryface planned to drive the king and his nobility and gentry from the country and clear off the forests, level the hills and make the whole state into a flat corn country. The king thought him simply a harmless old crank, and would listen to no warnings against him. But, nevertheless, the duke had a revolt well planned for the coming Fourth of July celebration. After bribing the bartenders, he had substituted raw sap for the mild and gentle aged liquors to be served on that day; he had the Cornmen all grandly inspired, and perfectly drilled, instructed and armed; though he had not converted the loggers, he had directed the bartenders to fill their glasses with triple-distilled, high-powered redeye sap on the night of the Fourth, and he was sure that he could capture them and keep them in bondage until the last whisky tree was felled. The duke did not fear Paul Bunyan, for he thought the loggers' stories about him to be drunken exaggerations; he thought of him as some plain leader whom they had basely deserted, and who would no doubt be happy to see them punished by slavery. He kept the strength and extensiveness of his power well hidden, and the loggers lived on blissfully in ignorance of their real danger.

For many days and nights after the stampede of his loggers Paul Bunyan had toiled on, swinging his timber scythe with undiminished rapidity. He had not observed the desertion of his men, or the flooding of his camp, or the fate of the stonewood trees. But at last his energy and strength began to fail, his pace slackened, he swung the scythe with slower strokes, and the intervals between the rolling thunders of falling trees became longer and longer. Then the timber scythe dropped from his hands, and he sank to the ground. Now he saw for the first time the shimmering distances of salt water which covered the stonewood trees and all but the tallest buildings of his camp. For seven hours he gazed on the lamentable scene, then his head dropped to the ground. He was not disheartened; he was only tired. He slept.

Days and nights went by with little change in the unnatural season. The days of springtime came, but here there was no spring. Summer days began, the sultriness of the nights got increasingly heavy and thick, and in the daytime the overpowering blaze of the sun seemed to make the very hills shrink, while the surface of the lake was veiled in steaming mists. The slumbers of Paul Bunyan, Johnny Inkslinger, the Big Swede and the blue ox became so deep that the active careers of all of them might have ended there ingloriously had it not been for Babe's appetite, which always tormented him, sleeping or waking. The Big Swede was couched on the high-piled hay in the manger, and Babe's chin rested on his body. Stirred by a hunger that would not be denied, his jaws began to work mechanically; they closed over the fifty pound plug of chewing tobacco that the Big Swede always carried in his hip pocket, and it was swallowed like a blade of grass. Babe gasped, groaned, and shuddered; then he lunged to his feet, snorting and bellowing, for chewing tobacco was as poisonous to him as to a circus elephant. He gouged the Big Swede viciously with his horns until he awoke with yells of agony and astonishment. And not until he saw, through the stable door, Paul Bunyan asleep on the far side of the lake did Babe heed the foreman's powerful remonstrances. With a last angry toss of his horns, which threw the Big Swede through the stable window, Babe turned and plunged into the water. So fast did he run that he threw foaming waves to the furthest reaches of the lake. When he reached Paul Bunyan he emitted a joyous bellow and eagerly began licking the great logger's neck. For one hour and twenty-seven minutes

Babe assiduously tickled him, and then Paul Bunyan sprang to his feet with a great roar of laughter. He felt strong and fresh; he smiled cheerfully at the blue ox, who capered around him. He straddled Babe and rode him across the lake to the flooded camp. There he awakened Johnny Inkslinger, and, refusing to listen to his apologies, he sent him out to discover the trail taken by the loggers. By the time it was found, Paul Bunyan and the Big Swede had the camp out of the water and ready to move. Babe was hitched to the buildings and the search for the errant loggers began. As he traveled on Paul Bunyan said nothing; his head was bowed in painful meditation. There was still wrath in his heart for his loggers' desertion of him, but there was more of loneliness. Excepting the pleasures of history-making, invention and oratory, there had never been any joy for him like the joy that comes from the comradeship of labor, and he wished to feel it again. Then he feared that the loggers might be completely lost; they were as helpless as sheep, without understanding guidance. One moment he swore to punish them severely, then his heart would be softened by sad and gentle thoughts. So engrossed was he with perplexing ideas and troubling emotions that he did not notice the decline of heat and the new sweetness in the air as the balmy clime of Kansas was approached. . . .

A Fourth of July in Topeka during the reign of King Bourbon! Who would not give his fame and fortune to have participated in one of those marvelous celebrations! What pale and weakly imitations we have nowadays of the ball games between the Fats and the Leans, of the potato races, and of all the other ingeniously devised contests which made the last day of King Bourbon's reign a long procession of glories and wonders! When will we see again parades, marches and drills performed by uniformed organizations as they were performed by The Bartenders' and Bookmakers' Bands, The Knights of the Spotted Cubes, The Mystics and Oracles of Fistiana, The Stentorian Order of Umpires, The Grandiose Guild of Jockeys, The Loyal Legion of Log-burlers and many others on that historical day in Topeka? The last-named society was a new organization that was composed of Paul Bunyan's loggers. They aroused the wildest enthusiasm when they appeared in the line of march treading beer kegs, and for this, and for their triumphs in the races, King Bourbon awarded them the grand prize.

The bar had been closed for the celebration, and when it was opened in the evening no one in the spruce and jocund throngs which streamed through its doors suspected that treason was afoot. Clinking of glasses, guffaws, jigging feet, back-slapping, bellowed songs and shouted jests made a tumult of rollicking and boisterous noise as the reveling began. Urged on by the traitorous bartenders, the nobility and gentry drank nothing but the sap of the whisky trees. It was a mild, mellow and soothing beverage when properly aged, but the raw green sap which the conspirators had supplied would suddenly addle the mind and paralyze the nerves. The loggers, flushed with conceit over their day's triumph, boasted that they were champion drinkers also, and they dared everyone to enter drinking contests with them. The bartenders, obeying instructions, filled the loggers' glasses with triple-distilled, high-powered redeye. So they were the first to get bleary-eyed, to wilt and to stagger about. By the time the nobility and gentry had begun to be affected the loggers had all stumbled outside or had been carried out. Too late the king and his followers realized that they were the victims of a conspiracy. When the fumes of the powerful green sap had completely befuddled them the spies of the Cornmen lighted the signal fires that were to start the attack.

In a short time the hosts of Cornmen, with husking hooks strapped to their left wrists, and with corn knives swinging from their right hands, charged, whooping and bounding, into the city. King Bourbon and his followers, deaf, weak-kneed, color-blind, dumb and addled, could make no resistance. They were driven through the streets, out of the city, on through the whisky tree forests and headed towards the far lands of Kentucky. Duke Dryface remained behind with the greater part of the Cornmen to secure the loggers, who were laid out in heaps, rows, circles, squares and fantastic groups all over the city. In three hours half of the loggers had balls and chains locked to their legs. Duke Dryface had begun to breathe easily and to enjoy the first glow of complete triumph when he became conscious of a vast shadow, an overpowering presence. The light of the moon seemed blotted out, the ground shook under a monstrous tread; then sounded a bellow of rage that lifted every Cornman and every logger seven feet into the air and whirled them all over five times before they struck the ground again. The rudely awakened and sobered loggers and the affrighted Cornmen then saw the august figure of Paul Bunyan and the blue ox looming above them. The good and mighty man was chiding Babe for bellowing so loudly and was restraining him from attacking the Duke and his followers.

Duke Dryface had the courage of true virtue. He fearlessly stepped up to Paul Bunyan and began a speech. First he spoke of the sins of King Bourbon and of the oppressions suffered by the Cornmen; he showed the necessity for reform. Next, he went on to prove that sin was in the very soil of Kansas, and that this soil could only be purified by destroying the evil forests and raising virtuous corn in their stead. That was his main reason for wanting to make slaves of the loggers, he said, but he hoped also to make righteous men of them later. Paul Bunyan nodded gravely for him to go on, and the duke then rose to the grandest heights of eloquence in describing the moral imperfections of the loggers. Deserters, braggarts, beer-bibbers, gluttons, cigarette fiends, and many other evil names he called them. Paul Bunyan listened, and the loggers got sick with shame and fear. They had surely sinned, they were indeed lost souls, they felt; they would forever despise themselves. Then, just when they had reached the lowest depths of self-loathing and despair, they saw Paul Bunyan give an enormous wink. Only a wink, but what forgiveness flashed from it, what unshakable faith seemed fixed in its depths! That one gesture of an eyelid restored and consoled them, for it spoke pardon and promised to forget. The duke declaimed until dawn, but the loggers listened complacently, grinning knowingly at each other. Once more they would toil grandly in the woods, once more hot cakes, ham and eggs would sizzle for them on the long kitchen ranges, once more they would be delighted by the wonders of noble Sunday dinners, for by the wink of his eye Paul Bunyan had made them his loggers again. . . .

Paul Bunyan contracted for the logging-off of the whisky trees, and this was easily accomplished by the inspired toil of the loggers. The country was flattened by hitching Babe to each section of logged-off land and then turning it over. As Duke Dryface had surmised, the land, though rolling on *top* was flat *underneath*. So the one-time sinful soil of Kansas now lies deeply buried, and only the barest vestiges of the grand life devised by King Bourbon survive anywhere in the Kansas country.

ORATORICAL MEDICINE

BEFORE the second season in the Hickory Hill country there had never been a great sickness in Paul Bunyan's camp. The health his loggers constantly enjoyed was due to the skill of Johnny Inkslinger, who was physician and surgeon, as well as timekeeper, to the good and mighty Paul Bunyan. His surgical feats were marvelous. When ears were bitten off, for example, in the playful jousts with which the loggers amused themselves, it was no trick for Johnny Inkslinger to sew them on tightly again. And when a logger got his face walked on by calked boots the timekeeper would fill the resulting cavities with bread crumbs, slap on some red paint, and the victim of play would return to the frolic, happy and unmarred. But it was digestive ills which he understood completely; for Paul Bunyan's loggers like the laborers and farmers of to-day, had most of their physical miseries in the mysterious regions about the stomach. His knowledge was gained by the most arduous study and extensive research. The timekeeper wrote reports and figured all day, he dosed the loggers and operated on them in the evening, and the night long he read doctor books. His Sundays and holidays he spent among the wild creatures of the forests and seas, and these he studied shrewdly and patiently. He examined fleas, he explored whales, he once found the bones of a

moose who had died of old age, and he tracked the
animal to its birthplace, noting all its habits and
methods of life on his way. His knowledge was
monumental and complete, but he was content to
remain a timekeeper in position and name.

In the second season on Hickory Hill the life of the
camp went on as usual for a long time. For twelve
hours each day the axes rang in the undercuts, the saws
sang through bark and grain, and there was everywhere
the death shudder, the topple and crashing fall of
lofty trees. The blue ox placidly snaked the logs to
the riverside, following the Big Swede, who, lost in
dreams every trip always walked on into the water.
The fumes and exhalations of the great cookhouse were
never richer with delightful smells. In the evenings
the bunkhouses were loud with gleeful roars as the
loggers punched and kicked each other in their pastimes. As the work went on Paul Bunyan grew
certain that this would be his greatest season among
the hardwoods. His heart warmed toward his men.
He planned for them feasts, revels, largesses, grand
rewards. All his thoughts were benevolent ones as he
directed operations. Then, at the height of his
record-breaking season, Babe, the blue ox, got a
misery.

It was a sly, slow, deceitful illness. It was first
marked in the decline of his sportiveness and affection.
It was his habit, when yoked and harnessed in the
morning, to make for the woods at a roaring gallop.
Always the Big Swede would grip the halter rope and

try to hold the blue ox to a walk; always Babe would plunge on, dragging the Big Swede after him; and always the dutiful foreman would hit the ground once in every ninety feet, yell, "Har noo!" and then be yanked into the air again, for Babe would pay no heed to the bouncing boss.   In the woods the blue ox always had to be closely watched, for he would chew up the trees in his jestful moments as fast as they were felled, and on the great drives he would prankishly drink the river dry, leaving the astounded rivermen mired in the mud of the stream bed.   He was forever gouging the Big Swede with his sharp horns or tickling Paul Bunyan's neck with his tongue.

When this playful spirit of his slackened and he began to walk slowly to the timber each morning, it was first thought to signify the approach of maturity, with its graver moods.   But when Paul Bunyan discovered him one day, standing with his front feet crossed, his head bowed, his cud vanished, and with tears rolling from his half-closed eyes, the great logger was alarmed.   He called Johnny Inkslinger from among his ledgers and ink barrels and ordered him to drop all other work until Babe's ailment was diagnosed and cured.

Though he had studied all animals exhaustively, Johnny Inkslinger had never practised veterinary medicine, except in treating Babe's inconsequential attacks of hayfever and asthma.   If he took the case he would be assuming a great responsibility, he told Paul Bunyan; he must have at least forty-seven hours to consider the matter.   The great logger, having due respect for the scientific temperament, granted him this, so the timekeeper retired to his office.

Paul Bunyan waited patiently, despite the fears and anguish that smote him when Babe looked at him with beseeching eyes.   Work had been stopped in the woods, and the anxious loggers spent most of their time around the stable.   The cooks, remembering Babe's fondness for hot cakes and fried eggs, brought him tubfuls of them most delicately cooked, but he would only nibble at them politely, then turn away. Once indeed his old jestful spirit returned when the Big Swede came near him.   He set his hoof on the foreman's foot, and at the anguished "Har noo!" he seemed to smile.   But what a difference there was between that shadow of merriment and the one time gay bellow that always followed the joke!   Paul Bunyan and the loggers were deeply touched.

Johnny Inkslinger finally announced in a scientific speech that he was prepared to examine and treat the blue ox.   He was certain, above all, that this illness was not caused by indigestion, for Babe's stomach had always seemed to be iron-clad, invulnerable.   When the hay supply ran low in the wintertime Paul Bunyan would tie a pair of green goggles over Babe's eyes and he would graze for weeks on the snow.   He was fond of the wires that bound his bales of hay, and he had always eaten them without apparent injury.   So Johnny Inkslinger ignored Babe's stomachs, but every other part of him, from muzzle to tail brush, was minutely scrutinized and explored.   Nothing escaped observation. Six intrepid loggers with lanterns were lowered by ropes into his throat to examine his tonsils when he stubbornly refused to say "Ah!" But no diseased condition could anywhere be discovered.

Johnny Inkslinger was baffled, but he would not give up. For sixty-one hours he sat in the stable, watching every movement of the blue ox and making pages of notes about each one. And all of the time he was thinking with the full power of his scientific mind, bringing all his vast medical knowledge to the solution of his problem. Then, just as he had reached the darkest depths of hopelessness, a flashing idea saved him with its light. The idea did not spring from his science or knowledge; indeed, it seemed to be in opposition to them. It was a simple idea, simply inspired.

His gaze had been fixed for some time on the hump which the blue ox had on his back. It was such a hump as all ailing animals contrive, but, unoriginal as it was, it was yet the source of an original and startling idea, that the hump in a sick animal's back, instead of being the *result* of the sickness, was really the *cause* of it! Johnny Inkslinger jumped to his feet with a shout of joy. He saw in the idea, not only the salvation of Paul Bunyan's logging enterprises, but the root of a great fame for himself as a veterinarian as well. His jubilant calls soon roused the camp.

Paul Bunyan listened somewhat doubtfully as the timekeeper revealed his idea and plans. But he was not one to oppose a scientific man with mere logic, so he gave orders that the great treatment devised by

Johnny Inkslinger should be carried out. For five days the loggers toiled, erecting a scaffold on each side of the blue ox. Runways were built from the top floors of the scaffolds to Babe's back. Then all was ready for the first treatment. For three hours loggers carrying pike poles, peavys, sledges and mauls climbed the scaffolds and extended in lines on each side of Babe's humped spine. Then Paul Bunyan grasped the horns of the sick creature, Johnny Inkslinger and the Big Swede seized his tail, the command, "Get ready!" was given, then, "Let's go!" Paul Bunyan said, and the army of doctors began the cure. All that day, through the night, and for seventy-six consecutive hours thereafter the loggers attacked the hump in Babe's spine, while Paul Bunyan, Johnny Inkslinger, and the Big Swede attempted to stretch it to its former shape by tugging on the poor animal's horns and tail. Babe mooed dolorously indeed while this treatment was being performed, and the tears rolled from his saddened eyes in foaming torrents. But he did not resist. Intelligent animal that he was, he knew that his friends were only trying to drive away his misery. And kindly of soul as he was, it was no doubt as much to give them the pleasure of success as to stop them from prodding, pounding and stretching his spine that he made a heroic effort to act as cured ox. Pretty deceiver! Once he had straightened his aching back, how lustily he began to devour bale after bale of bitter-tasting hay from his manger! How speedily he emptied tubfuls of hot cakes and fried eggs, while Hot Biscuit Slim, Cream Puff Fatty and the assistant

cooks looked on and cheered! Never did Babe depart more friskly for the woods than on the morning he was pronounced cured. The Big Swede, hanging to the halter rope, only hit the dirt once in every mile and a half!

The work of logging was soon in its old routine, but Paul Bunyan was not satisfied. Babe could not hide his spells of trembling; he moved feverishly; his expression was haggard, his mooings hollow. Johnny Inkslinger, still flushed with the fire of his grand idea, was impatient with Paul Bunyan's worriment. But he could not quiet the great logger's fears. When it was noted that Hickory River would suddenly rise three or four feet above its normal level and as suddenly fall again, Paul Bunyan set a close watch on the blue ox and discovered that there were times when the hump in his back became greater than ever before, and that torrents of tears often poured from his eyes in fits of weeping, thus flooding the river. Firmly, but without anger, Paul Bunyan ordered his timekeeper to devise another treatment.

Johnny Inkslinger reluctantly admitted his failure and again brought his powers of thought to consider the perplexing sickness of the blue ox. But he did not labor with the materials of his knowledge and science. He longed to glow again with the tickling heat of originality, to taste once more the sweet fat of his own ideas. So he sat and thought, awaiting inspiration, while his doctor books stood unopened on the towering shelves of the camp office. And at last he was rewarded by an idea that floated from mysterious darkness like a bubble of golden light. It was midnight, but his ecstatic shouts awakened the camp. The loggers, thrilled and alarmed, rolled from their bunks and ran in their underclothes to the camp office. A white-clad host soon filled the broad valley and covered the distant hills. Johnny Inkslinger then came out of the office, carrying a box that had held ninety-five tons of soap. He mounted this box and began to speak. His eyes flamed, his hair waved, his hands fanned the air. He was voluble. "Doctor or prophet?" Paul Bunyan asked himself sadly as he strode away, after listening for a short time. But the loggers were enchanted as the speech went on. Johnny Inkslinger ended each period with a mesmeric phrase, and after he had repeated it thrice at the ending of his speech the loggers made a chant of it. "Milk of the Western whale! Milk of the Western whale! Milk of the Western whale!" they roared, as they swayed and danced in their underclothes. The chant rose in thunders to the sky, it rolled over the hickory forests, and it shook the rocks of far mountains. It reëchoed for hours after the loggers had returned to the bunkhouses.

Paul Bunyan considered the situation bravely and calmly. He admitted no vain regrets that he had never studied doctoring himself. He pronounced no maledictions on his timekeeper's puzzling mania. He simply considered the plain facts of his problem: if Babe died the great logging enterprises would be halted forever; Johnny Inkslinger was the only man who had the science and knowledge to cure the sick ox, and if humored he might return to his senses; a change to the Western coast might benefit Babe, and the milk of the Western whale would surely do him no harm. So the mighty logger decided to move his camp to the West, and there let Johnny Inkslinger give him the whale's milk cure.

There was great rejoicing in the camp when Paul Bunyan gave orders for the move. The blue ox, seeming to realize that it was made for his benefit, acted as though he was in high spirits when he was hitched to the camp buildings and the bunkhouses loaded with loggers. He skipped and capered along the trail behind Paul Bunyan, Johnny Inkslinger and the Big Swede all the way to the Mississippi. But there he was attacked by innumerable squadrons of Iowa horse flies. He smashed them unmercifully with blows of his tail until the ground for miles around was strewn with their mangled bodies, but the carnivorous insects persisted in their assaults until Babe became blindly enraged. He lowered his head and began a furious charge that did not end until he reached Colorado, where he fell exhausted. The loggers had been made violently seasick by their bouncing journey over the hills, and Paul Bunyan was compelled to call a halt until they and the blue ox had recovered. While waiting, Paul Bunyan and the Big Swede built a landmark by heaping dirt around an upright pike pole, and the great logger was so pleased with the creation that he gave it a name, Pike's Peak.

The trip to the coast was made without further misadventures, and the loggers were set to work at once to build a whale corral, for Paul Bunyan wished to get the cure over as soon as possible, so that his stubborn timekeeper would begin to do some real doctoring. The loggers grumbled loudly at working with picks and shovels; such foreign labor demeaned them, they said. But the exhortations which Johnny Inkslinger delivered from his great soap box, and the alarming condition of the blue ox, who now made no effort to hide his sickness, but lay quietly, with closed eyes, overwhelmed their prejudices, and they made the dirt fly in spite of their dislike for shovels and picks. For nine days and nights they threw dirt like badgers, while Paul Bunyan and the Big Swede scooped it aside and piled it into big hills. Then the whale corral was finished, and Paul Bunyan sent the loggers to the bunkhouses. They were so sleepy and weary that they began to snore before they had put away their tools.

Paul Bunyan kicked a hole in the seaward side of the corral, and the waters of the Pacific roared into the basin. When it was filled he began his famous imitation of the bawl of a lonely whale, and so perfect was his mimicry that in less than an hour an approaching school of the leviathans was sighted. They swam hesitatingly about the opening to the corral for a time, but as Paul Bunyan continued to call ever more cunningly and appealingly, they at last entered the trap. The Big Swede then got his stool and milk bucket, while Paul Bunyan scooped dirt into the corral gate. Johnny Inkslinger was called from the office, and all was ready for the first milking of a creature of the seas.

The Big Swede, who had been raised on a dairy farm in the old country, selected a cow whale that looked like a good milker, and Paul Bunyan, using all his wiles of manner and tricks of voice, soon had her playing about his hands. At last she was gentle and quiet, and, while Johnny Inkslinger held up her tail, the Big Swede came into the water with his bucket and stool and began milking with all the energy and skill that had won him the name of Sweden's greatest milker in his youth. With the vigorous pressure of his hands, the whale's milk was soon gushing into his bucket with such force that a dozen fire engines could not have equaled the flow. The gentled whale made no resistance, and the pail was soon filled with healthful, creamy milk. But just as the Big Swede was about to rise from his stool the whale's calf, who had been swimming angrily about, suddenly charged the great milker and upset him. His head lodged in the milk bucket; he was bent double; and before he could recover himself, the little whale had butted the breath out of him and had spanked him blisteringly with his corrugated tail. This incident frightened the mother whale, and she escaped from Paul Bunyan's hands; the Big Swede floundered about and yelled from the depths of the milk bucket; and the whole school of whales plunged about the corral in a wild panic. Worst of all, the first milking was spilled.

And indeed they were the whole day securing one bucket of milk. Not until Paul Bunyan thought of letting a whale calf suck his finger while the Big Swede was milking its mother were the sea-going dairymen able to get away from the corral with one milking. But at last the great milker limped to the shore with a foaming pail. He was breathing in wheezes, his clothes were in tatters, and the back of him, from head to heels, was marked from the tail blows of the little whales. He was the sorriest of sorry sights, but he had a feeble smile, nevertheless, in return for Paul Bunyan's praise.

Babe took his first dose of whale's milk resignedly and then closed his eyes again in weariness and sighed with pain. Paul Bunyan's emotions smothered his caution; he ventured to express his doubts about the cure. Johnny Inkslinger immediately ran to the office, brought out his great soap box and mounted it.

"It is a nature cure!" he cried in ringing tones. "It cures slowly because nature cures slowly, but it cures surely and divinely! It is a great cure because it is a great idea, a marvelous idea, a heaven-sent idea, an original idea, my own idea, and it is the idea that will save us all!"

Paul Bunyan looked for a moment into the glowing eyes of his timekeeper and sighed. He did not reply.

For a week the three milked the whales twice daily and dosed the blue ox, while the loggers slept away their weariness. Babe took the whale's milk meekly, but at each successive dose he swallowed more sluggishly, and after the fourth day he would not open his eyes while he drank. On the day the loggers came from the bunkhouses he refused to drink at all. Only an occasional twitching of his eyelids showed that life yet remained with him.

"He is dying," said Paul Bunyan.

Johnny Inkslinger mounted the great box which had held the ninety-five tons of soap and began to speak.

"Fellow loggers and Paul Bunyan," he began. "This miraculous idea, this saving and transfiguring idea——"

"Silence!" commanded the good and mighty logger.

So compelling was the power of that grave and august voice that the loggers hardly breathed as it sounded, and the wind subsided until it made only the faintest whisper among the trees. Then Paul Bunyan made one of his great orations. He did not require a soap box, he made no fantastic gestures, and he spoke simply and smoothly. He reviewed his enterprises and the deeds of his loggers; he dwelt especially on the achievements and faithfulness of Babe, the blue ox. His plain sincerity held the loggers spellbound; for sixty-nine hours the speech went on, and they did not so much as move an eyelash. In conclusion, Paul Bunyan told them that Babe would surely die, and as logging could not be done without him, their last labor together would be to dig his grave. He did not blame Johnny Inkslinger, he said; the best of men may be led astray by their imaginings and fall into evil ways. He had been a great doctor once, and he was a noble scribe still. Then Paul Bunyan solemnly and warningly spoke of the shadowy workings of fate, and in somber utterance he portrayed the pathos of yearnings, the fraility of blessings and the ultimate vanity of all endeavor. In the last three hours of his oration his voice sounded as a tolling bell. Mournfully, mournfully, the moments marched on, and a darkness came over the hills and the sea. From the eyes of each motionless logger the tears streamed unchecked; they formed in puddles around each man's feet until all of them stood knee-deep in mud. When the oration was finished and they had extricated themselves and cleaned their boots, they made ready, and they left with Paul Bunyan for the North, where he had decided to dig Babe's grave. The Big Swede stayed with the dying ox, and Johnny Inkslinger hid himself in the shadows of his office.

For a long time he remained there in an agony of thought. Remorse tormented him, though Paul Bunyan had not judged him guilty. But he suffered most from the humiliation of failure. It was his first, but —the thought came like a blinding flash of light— had he failed—yet? His reservoir of ideas was inexhaustible; as long as breath remained in the blue ox he could try other ideas on him. Think now! It had become as easy for him to summon grand ideas as for a magician to conjure rabbits from a hat, and almost instantly he had one, a superb notion, a glorious thought!

Johnny Inkslinger rushed from the office and roused the Big Swede, who was sitting in apathetic sadness by the blue ox.

"Listen now!" commanded the timekeeper. "You are to sit here and repeat continuously in a soothing voice, 'You are well. You are well. You are well.' Do you understand? Well then—no questions now

—do as I have told you and Babe's life will be saved. Do not fail, for all depends on your faithfulness! When I have returned with Mr. Bunyan I will finish the cure myself."

The timekeeper, exulting in the certainty that his method would positively restore health to the blue ox, then started out on the trail of Paul Bunyan and the loggers. They should quit their melancholy task and return to find Babe on the road to recovery. He would complete the cure, and logging should go on as before.

The Big Swede at once began to repeat the words, "You ban well," according to orders. For thirty-one hours they came from his tongue without interruption. Then his mouth got dry and hoarseness invaded his throat. The phrase was uttered with an effort. Then he had to resort to whispering in Babe's ear. And finally even his whisper failed him.

The Big Swede had once nearly choked to death after making a high dive into muddy earth, and he had only been saved by copious doses of alcohol. The new oratorical cures were not understandable to him, but he remembered the potency of alcohol in clearing out the throat, so he got up and ran to the camp office, where he found the great carboys of the medicine once highly prized by Johnny Inkslinger. Taking three of them under his arm, the Big Swede returned to the blue ox. He took a huge drink from one of them, and he was again able to go on with the treatment. For a few hours it was only necessary for him to drink once every thirty minutes to drive away the hoarseness, but it resisted stubbornly, and the periods between the drinks grew shorter and shorter. By the time the Big Swede had opened the last carboy of alcohol his brain was addled by the fumes of the liquor, and his heart was softened by its influence until it beat only with sympathy for the blue ox. He forgot what he was to say, and instead of repeating, "You ban well," he began to sigh, over and over, "Poor ol' sick feller. Poor ol' sick feller." Fortunately this horrid perversion of Johnny Inkslinger's idea did not last. The Big Swede's vocal cords finally gave out, the alcohol smothered his will and closed his eyes. He could not resist the fogginess that crept over his brain, and at last he fell over and began to snore.

Babe had lain motionless and silent while the Big Swede was treating him, but when the foreman fell he had knocked over the last carboy of alcohol, and the liquor poured over the nostrils of the blue ox and trickled into his mouth. He groaned, he stirred, his legs quivered. Then he sat up, looking eagerly about for more. He soon spied, through the open door of the office, the glitter of the other containers of liquor. Slowly, painfully, he staggered to his feet. His tongue lolling feverishly, he stumbled towards the office. A desperate swing of his horns crashed in the side of the building, a flirt of his hoofs knocked the tops from the remaining carboys, and in nineteen minutes he had emptied them all. A vat of Epsom salts was cleaned up in seven gulps, barrels of pills and capsules, and cartons of powders were quickly devoured; in half an hour there was nothing left of the old time medicines of Johnny Inkslinger but splinters and broken glass.

Then the alcohol began to surge through the veins of the blue ox. The frisky, exuberant spirit of his healthy days returned. He pranced and sashayed. He lifted his tail and bellowed. His breath came in snorts as he lightly pawed the ground. For a time he was content with such merry gamboling, frolicking and romping about, then he felt a sentimental longing for Paul Bunyan and his mates of the woods, and he started out to find them. But the alcohol mounted to his head, it dimmed his eyes, and he lost the trail. He wandered into the Wet Desert country and was caught in a terrific rainstorm. He toiled stubbornly on, though his befuddled senses had lost all sense of direction and he sank knee-deep into the desert mud at every step. As he struggled ahead, weaving first to the right, then to the left, then to the right again, water rolled from his back and foamed in cataracts down his dragging tail. A river coursed down the crooked path he left behind him. He grew weak again after he had plowed through the mud for hours and the fever had left his blood. When the storm passed his strength left him and he sought rest on a high plateau.

There Paul Bunyan and the loggers found him, after a three weeks' search which had begun when the Big Swede brought the news of his disappearance. At first the loggers were sure he was dead, and groans of sorrow rose in dismal thunders from the vast host. But Johnny Inkslinger would not give up hope. He had repelled the lure of grand ideas at last, and he had his old medicine case with him now. In a moment he had emptied its store of alcohol and Epsom salts down Babe's throat. In a few minutes the blue ox opened his eyes. The loggers frantically cheered. Babe answered them with a bellow that threw even the loggers on the farthest hills to the ground. Though the blue ox was thin and feeble still, the vitality of health was in his voice again. "He is cured!" said Paul Bunyan.

"He is cured!" shouted the loggers, as they scrambled to their feet.

"Yah," said the Big Swede blissfully.

Johnny Inkslinger alone said nothing. He, too, was cured.

Say the old loggers:

Ever since he took his drunken course through the Wet Desert a stream has flowed down the crooked trail made by the blue ox. It is called Snake River in all the geographies. The great whale corral is known as Coos Bay. And Babe's unfinished grave has become the islands and waters of Pugent Sound. The Cascade Mountains of Washington were made from the dirt thrown up by the loggers and Paul Bunyan when they began to dig the grave, and a bitter dispute still rages regarding the name for the loftiest peak. The loggers and the people of Seattle call it Mt. Bunyan, the people of Tacoma and the Indians call it Mt. Tacoma, and the geographers and tourists have named it Mt. Rainier, after the weather, which is rainier there than in any other part of the country.

So say the old loggers.

And loggers are truthful men.

NEW IOWA

PAUL BUNYAN, a historian first, an industrialist second, an inventor third, an orator fourth, was perhaps an artist in the fifth degree of his importance. Most authorities among the loggers of to-day insist that he was a great man of only four parts; they declare there was no art in him. The authorities of the classroom, less reverent and generous in their judgments, refuse to consider him as more than an industrialist; but the professors must be doubted a little, because they are certainly jealous of the great logger's simple eloquence and his popularity with the plain people.

In the camps I have heard college loggers quote a teacher whom they called Professor Sherm Shermson as follows: "Fellows, there is no use talking. Paul Bunyan was a conscientious logger, I guess. Maybe he wrote *big* histories but, fellows, he didn't write *great* histories. And his inventions were only useful in his logging operations; not one of them has become a universal boon to humanity. I expect he could make a right good speech; but, mark this point now, there is a *difference* between a right good speech and eloquence. Eloquence, fellows, must have morals and ideals in it to *be* eloquence. And as Paul Bunyan had French-Canadian blood, I must believe that his orations had more of Latin emotionalism in them than of Real American ideals and morals. I guess we'll agree, fellows, that his Nordic foreman was a man of greater moral force and of purer mind."

I do not know the rest of the professor's argument, as the college loggers would listen to no doubts against the teachings of Professor Sherm Shermson. So I would always leave them when they went too far in their educated talk. Some might think that Professor Sherm Shermson was misquoted by his boys; but the first thing college loggers hear when they come to the woods is warnings about the dangers of telling falsehoods in the bunkhouses; so it is probable that the words which they attribute to Professor Sherm Shermson are typical of the teachings about Paul Bunyan in American universities.

But so long as trees are felled the race of loggers will hold to a staunch faith in Paul Bunyan as the supreme historian and maker of history, the most resourceful inventor, and the most powerful orator, as well as the most enterprising industrialist of all time. But they too question his art. He appreciated the folk songs and tales of his men, it is admitted, and he had his playhouses, wherein he painted and sculped about. His Paint Pots are still to be seen in the Yellowstone, and his wall painting in the Grand Canyon shows that he was clever with the brush. Most of his sculpture was left unfinished, but it is impressive, for all that. His beginnings for the busts of Johnny Inkslinger and the Big Swede, the unfinished works in the Yosemite which are called North Dome and Half Dome, plainly show that he was no crude

chiseler.   But, it is no wonder that loggers have little
to say about their hero's artistic creations, for these
works had nothing to do with the logging industry, and
he had no help from his men in making them.   He
only amused himself with art when he had no difficult
labors to perform.   Then, it is known that he opposed
the teaching and practice of art among his loggers.
He was particularly opposed to the writing of poetry
by his men.   He encouraged the making of simple
songs and the telling of true tales by picked men, bunkhouse bards; but even these favored minstrels dared
not attempt the making of grand, grave and lofty
verse.

The earnest and reverent critic who studies Paul
Bunyan will come to reason, however, that the master
logger's Camp Rule 31,721, which prohibited the writing of poetry, is no fair indication of his own feeling
for noble rimes; it only proves that he thought his
loggers no more fitted for the enjoyment of art than
they were fitted for the understanding of history or
the comprehension of scientific inventions.   It is very
probable that Paul Bunyan himself wrote tragic blank
verse in his exuberant youth, and happy hunting songs
in his elder years of discouragement.   But he kept
them to himself.   He felt that all art was dangerous
for his loggers; he knew that poetry was especially so.
This he learned in his attempt to log off New Iowa.
For there the loggers all turned poets and nearly
ruined the logging industry.

Paul Bunyan's decision to move to New Iowa developed from the thought that its healing climate

would hasten the convalesence of Babe, the blue ox, and that its orange palms would give his men the tough logging which they sorely needed. Babe, having fallen sick, had been near to perishing from Johnny Inkslinger's new-fangled cures; but he was saved when the camp doctor got sense and returned to his old-fashioned reliable remedies. The blue ox was now cured, but he was far too weak to begin hard labor at once. So his master was put to it to devise a plan that would let Babe regain his strength and yet give natural labor to the loggers.

Since leaving the Hickory Hill country, they had done little of the grand work for which they were born. They had lost a great deal of their innocent pride and self-respect in toiling with picks and shovels; and Johnny Inkslinger's abandonment of scientific medical practice for medical oratory had shaken their faith in the integrity of his knowledge and the scope of his power. In the time when he had written his figures and made his cures without explaining and glorifying them the loggers had regarded him as a worker of mysteries and had been in great awe of him. But now that he had revealed his mind from a soap box the loggers only remembered his eloquent boasts and his failure to make good. Alcohol and Epsom salts seemed common to them now, and they laughed at the camp doctor for having had to go back to them.

Paul Bunyan heard them poking rough fun at Johnny Inkslinger's folly on their first night in the Oregon camp, after the return was made from the Wet Desert country.

"In words there is a magic poison which is more powerful than the plain substance of them," mused Paul Bunyan. "This magic whips emotions and stuns sense, and it overpowers any mind which is one part sense and nine parts emotion. And these loggers of mine . . . these loggers of mine. . . ."

Another clamor broke out in the bunkhouses, and Paul Bunyan, smiling sadly, listened to hear what nonsense his men were talking now. The bunkhouse cranks were the leaders in the new uproar, and when the master logger heard their words and the applause that followed, his eyebrows drew down in a frown which the moonlight could not penetrate, and his eyes had a hard glitter in the shadows.

For the bunkhouse cranks were saying that it looked like logging couldn't last much longer now; the old blue ox was in a bad way and it was hard to think he'd ever be himself again in this here world; Johnny Inkslinger was getting so childish that he'd probably lose his figuring power, just as he had blundered in his doctoring; and old Paul himself—it looked like even he was losing his hold, as he had started to dig Babe's grave before the blue ox was even near dead. Old Paul would never have given in that soon in the days on Onion River, said the bunkhouse cranks. Things would surely go from bad to worse, they agreed, and it was no use to look for the good old times to come back. The same talk was going on in all the bunkhouses and the bards had few cheerful arguments against it. The loggers were losing their old innocent, exuberant, devil-may-care spirit.

Paul Bunyan sat down on six of the high hills above the whale corral, pulled up a young fir tree and began to brush his beard and ponder. He had no doubts of his own powers and he felt that Johnny Inkslinger was as great as ever. The timekeeper's recent obsessions and eccentricities were due to the lowness of spirit, the stagnation of soul, which comes sometime to all mental men. He was now recovered, and he would certainly do his part in the making of logging history as well as before, perhaps better. The trouble now was with the loggers. True men of muscle, the best virtues for them to possess were unquestioning loyalty and faithfulness to their leaders and simple confidence in them. Oratory was good for them when it stimulated these virtues, but ideas were poisonous; for they caused the loggers to become critics and independent thinkers, and their minds were not fitted for such occupations.

"Work and discipline will repair the damage," decided Paul Bunyan. "Work is the great consoler, for in it men forget the torments and oppressions of life. And nothing is more tormenting and oppressive to men of muscle than ideas. My loggers shall forget them. And strong discipline shall release them from the troublous responsibilities of independence. Again I shall have a camp of men who toil mightily and make the hours between supper and sleep jolly with merry songs and humorous tales."

Saying this, Paul Bunyan rose and looked over the fir forest which covered all the hills and threw shadows far over the silent waters of the whale corral. The great logger regretted that he could not remain here and fell these splendid trees; but something more than plain logging was needed for his present purpose. A powerful task must be set for his men, but a task that would not require arduous labor from the blue ox. New Iowa best suited his need. There the climate was as healing and mild as the one which Kansas had possessed before the turnover of its sinfulness. Paul Bunyan's maps showed that New Iowa had great forests of orange palms in its valleys, and his samples proved that these trees were tough cutting. The start for the New Iowa country should be made at once.

Paul Bunyan went first to the camp office and called out the Big Swede. He gave orders for Babe to be harnessed and hitched to the camp buildings; then he called, "Roll out or roll up!" for the loggers. They came out slowly, rubbing their eyes and expressing wonder, for they had been sleeping only a short while. When their leader told them that he was going to take them down to New Iowa they did not display their usual childish excitement over a move; but they looked from one to another with knowing grins and much eye-winking. The bunkhouse cranks whispered, "Ol' Paul's off on another wild goose chase"; and some of the boldest among them declared that they had never seen better logging than the Oregon country offered, and if they had their way about it they'd stay right here.

Paul Bunyan did not reprove them for their doubts and impertinent remarks. With a shrewd show of patience and forbearance, he made them a speech in which he cunningly portrayed their unreasoning enthusiasm for Johnny Inkslinger's new cures. Had it not been for their applause, the timekeeper would have quickly abandoned his unscientific notions, Paul Bunyan said, and the recent troubles would have been avoided. He hoped they had learned a lesson, the leader continued, that they would never again look for hurtful ideas in speeches, but for excitement, jollity and contentment only, as that was the best that oratory could give them. Their business was not to think, but to fell trees. They were, beyond a doubt, the greatest tribe of loggers that would ever march through the woods, he said in conclusion, and as Paul Bunyan's men they would have glory in history. But as thinkers they were no better than prattling children.

"Back to your bunks!" ordered the leader-hero. "And I want no more nonsense from you about ideas."

The loggers, blushing with shame and contrition, were quick to obey; and they all crawled under their blankets and hid their red faces. The Big Swede had the buildings wired together by this time; the blue ox was hitched to the cookhouse; Paul Bunyan, the foreman, and the timekeeper took hold of the traces to help pull the long load, and the start for New Iowa was made.

Babe had a hard pull over the mountains, and, with all the help that was given him, he labored slowly up the slopes. He was wearied out when the Tall Timber country was reached at dawn. Paul Bunyan stopped for a rest, and the loggers came out to gaze upon the trees whose tops were as lofty as the clouds.

The great logger himself was delighted to find trees that towered far above his head, and he got an over-powering desire to try an ax and a saw on them. Here were trees that were too tall and large for his loggers to work on; this timber was made for him and it offered him the chance for the historical individual logging accomplishment that he had always dreamed about.   Paul Bunyan swore loudly that, redeemed loggers or no redeemed loggers, cured ox or uncured ox, he would send the camp on in charge of the Big Swede and the timekeeper and enjoy a holiday of pow-erful, pleasant labor.   So he set up his workshop and built himself a crosscut saw that would span even the largest trunks, he made a regulation felling ax of a size to fit his hands, and he devised some wedges from Babe's old ox shoes.

The next morning the camp was started on its way again; and as it left the Tall Timber country the log-gers looked back on the vanishing figure of their hero-leader, and their eyes got dim, and a doleful loneliness whispered in all their hearts.

"Paul Bunyan's a good and mighty man," they said sincerely.

Happily, New Iowa was a country of such enchant-ing colorful aspect that the loggers were consoled when the camping place on Lavender River was reached. There had lately been considerable argument in the bunkhouses as to whether Kansas before the turnover of sinfulness was not a more ideal country than that around the old home camp.   But here was a land which seemed to surpass both regions.   The blue of the sky looked as though it had been painted there, and the hills, too, huge heaps of daisies, bluebells, poppies and buttercups, were out of a picture-book. The river got its name from its lavender color, and its unblemished stream curved delicately through the forests of orange palm, and the meadows of pink clover, which were like vast but dainty rugs on the valley floor. Pale green moss hung over the river banks to hide any ugliness of soil, and mauve and lemon blooms of water lilies made a lovely variance of color in the lavender water. The orange palms were as tall as coconut palms, and they resembled them in shape also. The foliage, blossoms and fruit were all in the thick crests of the tree tops; the leaves and blooms were like those of the common orange trees of to-day; the bark of some of the trees was purple, on others it was gold, and a few had bark which was wine-red. All were now in heavy bloom, and the forests were roofed with solid masses of white blossoms, for the orange palms stood so close together that a logger could hardly squeeze between their trunks.

All that day Paul Bunyan's loggers wandered about, savoring the deliciousness of the scene; at suppertime they could not eat, for the odors of beans and stewed onions were repugnant, after breathing the heavy-sweet fragrances of the drowsy New Iowa air. Nor could they enjoy songs and stories that evening, for they still heard the canaries singing among the orange blossoms. Neither could they sleep, for their honest blankets seemed tough and unclean after their rollings of the day on the pink clover and the daisies and buttercups.

But there was no poetry in the Big Swede's soul, and he called them out at sunup with a vulgar "Roll out or roll up, by yeeminy!" He only thought of the job before him, and he was out to show Paul Bunyan that the camp had been left in capable hands.

The loggers, beguiled by the charms of their new delicacies, all shaved and donned clean underclothes before they came out to work, and the Big Swede growled at them for being late.

"We gat bum yob har noo," he said. "We gat swamp har first, for, by yeeminy, these trees too close for fall noo. You gat broosh hooks; climb tree; an' aye tank you better swamp first noo. Aye gas so."

The Big Swede was in a tremble from his greatest oratorical effort, and he hastened to give the blue ox some hay, that he might recover his composure. When he had returned, the loggers were moving slowly for the forests, each man carrying a brush hook over his shoulder. When they reached the orange palms each man selected a tree and climbed it; and by noon thousands of purple, gold and wine-red trunks were bare and glittering in the sun, their tops swamped away. The ground around them was piled six feet high with blossom-laden boughs. This, though the loggers had swamped languidly.

For a week the swamping went on with fair progress, and the Big Swede rejoiced in the thought that he was so conducting operations that Paul Bunyan would give him high praise.

Then the loggers spent their first Sunday of indolence in this hyacinthine land. Hot Biscuit Slim, alarmed by the piles of uneaten food which were left on the tables from each meal, prepared a grand feast; he and the baker and their helpers used their skill to the utmost on it; but it was a vain effort, for at dinnertime not one diner appeared. The loggers had all flocked over the hills, and they were now swimming in the waters of the Southern Sea—those warm, crystal waters which lapped languorously on the golden strands of New Iowa. And the loggers got pink and white sea shells, and when they heard the soft music of them they began dancing, and when sundown came they were singing also. Prancing and warbling, they returned to camp in the moonlight, forgetting their clothes.

Imagine now the wrath and perplexity of the Big Swede next morning when he saw the loggers running nakedly about, hopping, skipping and posing. He roared at them till they remembered their work and recovered their boots and clothes from the seashore; but when they were once more aloft in the orange palms they swamped off few of the blossom-laden boughs. Instead, most of them brought out pencils and paper and began to write.

It is certain that Paul Bunyan would never have sent his camp to New Iowa if he had known that its scenery would evoke longings to write poetry in even the simplest souls, thus taking their energies from useful labor. The loggers could not be blamed; for a week now they had been tramping back and forth through piles of orange blossoms which reached to their armpits; a sky of painted blue had glittered above them; lavender waters, pale green banks, pink meadows, hills of daisies, bluebells, poppies and buttercups had bewitched them also; and the honied melodies of canaries had poured into their ears from dawn to dusk each day. The devil himself, coming to such a land, would throw down his pack of sins and temptations and sit upon it to think out a sonnet.

But the Big Swede had no soul, and the loggers' abandonment of labor puzzled and angered him. He yelled at them until some were shaken from the trees. But not one lost his pencil and paper. Johnny Inkslinger, hearing the uproar, left off his figuring and delivered an oration; but the loggers went on writing dreamily, paying no heed to the timekeeper.

"You will have to give them up," he said to the Big Swede. "It's a case which only Mr. Bunyan can handle."

He went back to his ledgers, and the foreman reluctantly set out for the Tall Timber country. The Big Swede found Paul Bunyan in such happiness over his labor that it seemed evil to tell him disturbing news. The great logger had all the tall trees felled by now and he was grubbing out the stumps. He was at work on the last row of them when the Big Swede found him.

"Needing me already?" he asked jovially. "Well, first help me drag out these stumps, then tell me your difficulties."

He said this, seeing the embarrassment of the Big

Swede and hoping to make him easy in mind. The two mighty men then tackled the row of stumps, and in a short time they were uprooted, leaving an enormous chasm, the chasm which in this day is called Yosemite.

"Now, there is a historical accomplishment for all to read about," said Paul Bunyan, with great satisfaction.

Followed by his foreman, he then strode over to the Bay and washed away the stains of toil. This done, he sat down and began to brush his beard with a young redwood tree.

"Now I will listen to you," he said.

The Big Swede's account of the loggers' strange doings astonished him. The foreman had said nothing about their writing, for he had never heard of poetry and had hardly noticed the papers and pencils in the loggers' hands.

"Aye tank dey yoost gat lazy noo," he said, nodding sagely.

"I hope it is nothing worse," said Paul Bunyan. "Laziness I can cure. But come; we must reach New Iowa before sundown."

The two great men traveled swiftly, and they reached the orange palm forests just as the sun was touching fluffy clouds on the Western horizon. The loggers, gathered in the meadows around the camp, were reading aloud from pages which they held in their hands. They did not observe the approach of their leaders, and when Paul Bunyan got within hearing distance of them he stopped and listened.

"Blossoms, white blossoms! Oh, orange palm blossoms!
My heart is afloat on a sea of white blossoms;
My heart is a-cry with the calls of canaries;
My heart is a-swoon with the odor of clover"

This was the shouting of one logger.
Another's roar sounded above the many:

> "A snow of daisies on the hill,
>   White drifts all starred with gold.
> But, ah, such snow wilt never chill—
>   It never makes thee cold."

This logger went on yelling about a rain of buttercups that would not make you wet, and a soft hail of
poppy petals, and a wind of bluebells; but by and by
he seemed to get mixed up and his voice got hoarse.
Then another logger made himself heard above the
tumult of bawled rhythms.   He cried:

> "From Onion River did I come,
>   Seeking a sweet opprobrium,
> A glorious derogatory
>   For my rare lust and allegory.

> "When I reached this dear venial state,
>   How my heart did debilitate!
> It leered, it fleshed, it energized,
>   But its emulsion I disguised.

> "I doffed among the daisies snide
>   Till their wan petals mortified.
> Egregious as incessant Noah,
>   I swamped in carnal New Iowa."

"Poetry!" gasped Paul Bunyan. "Thunderation! Holy mackinaw!"

But the loggers did not hear him, and Shanty Boy, the great bunkhouse bard, now made himself heard above the din.

> "Oho! I am a bully boy,
> I come from Thunder Bay
> At Pokemouche and Sault au Cochon
> I got the right o' way."

"That's more truth than poetry," murmured Paul Bunyan, somewhat mollified. He waited to hear more of this piece which sounded like a bunkhouse ballad; but now Bab Babbitson, who had heretofore been looked upon as a useless fussbudget around the camp, began to read his poem. He had the loudest voice of anyone among the common men, and the other loggers stopped their own reading to listen to him.

He bellowed:

> "Here is the land of opportunity.
> It is a sun-kissed land.
> Flowers bloom on the hills.
> The sun shines every day.
> The fruit grows thick on the trees and a man
> Can pick his breakfast off the trees every morning.
> People will want to buy farms here some day.
> Let's organize a company and sell shares.

> "Here is the land of opportunity.
> It is a sun-kissed land.
> Flowers bloom on the hills.
> The sun shines every day.

Here are pink meadows along a lavender river.
They would make wonderful townsites.
People will want to buy lots here some day.
Let's organize a company and sell shares.

"Here is the land of opportunity.
It is a sun-kissed land.
Flowers bloom on the hills.
The sun shines every day.
And I'd bet good money there's oil in this country.
Anyway, it's a wonderful place to dig for it.
People will want to get in on the ground floor some day.
Let's organize a company and sell shares.

"Yes, this is the land of opportunity.
People will come here from all over some day
To buy farms, lots, climate and oil wells.
Let's organize a company and sell shares."

The loggers all nearly fell over when they heard
this; they were tremendously surprised, for they had
never imagined that Bab Babbitson could have it in
him. They hid their own poems, for they were
ashamed of them now, and someone lifted a shout,
"Hurrah for Bab Babbitson, the boss poet of Paul
Bunyan's camp!" Everyone cheered and begged for
more verses. Bab Babbitson, gloriously puffed up,
was about to comply, when the loggers saw two great
shadows advancing upon them. They looked up and
beheld Paul Bunyan and the Big Swede. The great
logger's brows were drawn in a terrible frown, and his
beard was shaking from his rage as the forest boughs
shake when a swift wind blows among them.

"Are these Paul Bunyan's loggers?" he roared. "I don't recognize them!"

The poets were all tumbled from their feet by the force of that wrathful voice, and all but Bab Babbitson lost their poems in the scramble.

"Where are my old comrades of labor?" their leader went on more gently. "Where are the happy bunkhouse gangs that told loggers' tales and sang loggers' songs after their honest twelve hours of labor were done? Are you still loggers, or have you really degenerated into poets?"

They were shamed and they did not answer; but just then Johnny Inkslinger came out of his office and told Paul Bunyan of the terrible effect which the climate and scenery of New Iowa had on the soul after some living in it.

"Then it is no country for loggers," declared Paul Bunyan.

He ordered the Big Swede to make the camp ready for an immediate move, and he sent his men to the bunkhouses.

Then he took the felling ax he had devised for the tall timbers, and through the forests of orange palms he strode, smashing them into splinters. Kicks from his calked boots tore up the pink meadows and filled the lavender river with mud. Next, he demolished the hills, leaving them in scattered piles of barren sand. He regretted that he could not dissolve the climate also, thus banishing forever the enervating prettiness of the land. But he felt that he had done a good night's work as it was.

"So much for New Iowa," he said at last, with a sigh of weariness and content.

In the dark hour before dawn the camp was speeding Northward. But Bab Babbitson was not in his bunkhouse. Still clutching his poem, he had slipped out ere the start was made and hid in the forest wreckage. He was the one man in all that mighty host who was not a born logger. And now he had found his own country.

THE HE MAN COUNTRY

In Paul Bunyan's time the He Man country was far from its present tame and safe condition. It was then a high, smooth valley which lay between the Cascade Mountains and the Rockies. The highest peaks towered only a few hundred feet above it. Down the center of the valley Moron River flowed, and on each side of this amazing stream the sage trees grew, the wild horses roved, and the long-eared, stub-tailed high-behinds sat with lifted front feet and savagely sniffed the air for the scent of their hereditary enemy, the blond wolf. There, too, the tigermunks lifted their tails and screamed in the moonlight. The professors maintain that the tigermunks, the blond wolves and the high-behinds got their great size from eating prune pits which were thrown out from Paul Bunyan's cookhouse, and that they were all shot by the settlers who followed the great logger. This notion is ridiculous. The truth is that these animals were cowards at heart, and . . . But this should be told at the end of the story.

Paul Bunyan moved to this region after his disastrous experience in New Iowa, when his loggers all turned poets. He depended on the He Man country to make plain, honest men of them again. The supermasculine sage trees, he was sure, would inspire them to anything but poetry; and the logging off of these hard forests would be a historical achievement. But the great logger left nothing to chance. He remembered a species of animal which his boss farmer, John Shears, had originated, and he ordered a herd of them to be brought West. John Shears had proved to him that the virility of buffalo milk was incomparable. So Paul Bunyan planned to stuff his loggers with buffalo milk hot cakes as an antidote to any poison of poetry that might remain in them.

Thus the great logger's first move in the He Man country was to build a great buffalo corral and milking pen. When it was completed the buffalos were brought from the old home camp, and a gang of scissor-bills came along to herd and milk them. After their first breakfast of the new man food the loggers got some of their old swagger back, and Paul Bunyan was a picture of cheerfulness as he cruised the sage trees and planned the work of his men.

Moron River offered a chance for the most eventful and picturesque drive of logging history. From its source above the Border to its mouth on the Oregon coast it was like a huge child of a river, for it flowed ridiculously in every mile of its course. Here it ran smoothly for a short distance, then it would flow jerkily, making spasmodic waves; again, its surface would form into vast eddies that whirled like merry-go-rounds, and from these the waters rushed in heaving rolls of foam; there were quicksands where the river played hide and seek, nearly disappearing in places, miles where it turned and ran back and then curved into its course again, making a perfect figure eight.   Moron River flowed everywhere in zigzags and curlicues, cutting all manner of capers and didos. Any man but Paul Bunyan would have admitted the impossibility of making a drive on it.   But he only smiled when he saw it and said: "If my rivermen will forget poetry they can drive it easily."

The timber in this high, wide valley reached from the Eastern slopes of the Cascade Hills to the Western slopes of the Rockies.   These sage trees resembled the desert sagebrush of to-day.   They were not large; few of them were over two hundred feet in height, and not one of them could give a butt log over nine feet in diameter.   But they all had many massive limbs which were crowded with silver gray leaves, each leaf being the size of a No. 12 shoe.   The brown bark of the sage trees was thick, loose and stringy; it would have to be peeled from the logs before they were snaked to the landings by the blue ox.

"Splendid work for the swampers and limbers," said Paul Bunyan, as he cruised the timber.   "What a noble logging land is the He Man country!   Surely my loggers will be re-born here into even better men than they were before they fell into an illness of poetry and ideas!"

The first day of logging in the He Man country seemed to justify the great logger's best hopes.   The men came out from breakfast with a swinging, swaggering tramp, loudly smacking their lips over the lingering flavors of buffalo milk hot cakes.   This potent food made them vigorously he in every action.

Each man chewed at least three cans of Copenhagen and a quarter-pound of fire cut during his first twelve hours in the woods. "P-tt-tooey! P-tt-tooey! P-tt-tooey!" sounded everywhere among shouted oaths and coarse bellowing. Every ax stroke buried the bit deeply in the tough sage wood, and brown dust spurted and gushed constantly from every singing saw. Crash! Crash! Crash! The thunder of falling trees sounded like a heavy cannonade. On all the loggers' backs gray sweat stains spread from under their suspenders, and their hair hung in dripping strings over their red, wet faces. They had got up steam for the first time since leaving the Hickory Hill country, and they were rejoicing in it. Even after the eleventh hour had passed their eyes were bright, though red-rimmed from stinging sweat, though wrinkles of weariness had formed around them. The men were tired indeed; the fallers and swampers were now panting through open mouths, and they were chewing nervously on their tongues, as is the habit of men when they are wearied out; but they never missed a lick, and when Paul Bunyan called them home they could still walk springily.

When they were back in camp they did not even complain of the smeared, sticky feeling which always follows great sweats. No one spoke delicately of bathing; the loggers all washed and combed carelessly; and soon they made a trampling, growling host around the cookhouse door.

The rafters and beams of the great cookhouse shook at this supper, so savagely did the loggers tackle the platters of bear meat.   Even the bones were crushed, ground, and devoured; and Hot Biscuit Slim and his helpers were delighted when all the dishes were left slick and clean.

That night no poems were recited in the bunkhouses, but the loggers roared out "The Jam on Garry's Rock" and other plain old songs.   The loggers all crawled into their blankets at an early hour, and every one of them emitted gruff snores as soon as he went to sleep.

Paul Bunyan listened to them, and he praised the saints for the He Man country.   Had it not been for this region there was no telling what continuous plagues of poetry would have afflicted his simple men. Now they were back to normalcy.

The loggers continued to improve as summer passed and the short autumn of the He Man country ran its course.   The first snow of the cold season fell on a redeemed camp.   That snow flew in on a thundering wind; its flakes quickly made masses of dry snow around the bunkhouse doors; and these were swept into huge drifts that were window-high in places when the breakfast gong rang.   The loggers roared and cheered when they rushed out for their buffalo milk hot cakes.   Paul Bunyan listened to their basso growls of hunger, their rumbling jovial cursing, their bellows of laughter, and he chuckled so heartily that the snow which had gathered on his beard was shaken over a crowd of loggers, burying them.   They dug themselves out, whooping their appreciation of the humorous happening, and they jestfully shook their fists at their chuckling leader.   Then, without stopping to dig the snow from their shirt collars, they galloped on for the steaming cookhouse.

The stamping and banging, the clatter and crash, the smoking, sucking and grinding of meal time had never sounded with more vigor and power than on this wild winter morning. Breakfast done, the loggers came forth wiping their mouths with flourishing swipes of their fists, and with much snorting thumb-blowing of noses. When they were back in the bunkhouses, they laced up their boots, arguing loudly the while as to whether true savages, real tough bullies, would wear mackinaws when it was only forty below zero.

"Mackinaws?" yelled the majority. "Where's your red bully blood, you Hunyoks? Mackinaws! Hell, no, burlies; we won't even button the collars of our shirts!"

And then Ford Fordsen, camp tinker, bunkhouse handyman, and prophet, got an idea which swiftly ran through all the bunkhouses.

"Real rough, red-blooded, burly, bully, savage, dirt-stomping, ear-chewing, tobacco-loving, whisker-growing, hell-roaring He Men are not going to wear their boots and pants like we've been doing," said he. "Look you now: here's a ten-inch boot top, here are two inches of wool sock above it; and there's a pants' leg all tucked down nice and pretty inside of it. Mates, it looks too delicate. It is no way for a fire-eating logger to wear his duds. Here now; watch me and do as I do, and be a real band of honest-to-God bullies. This way—look!"

He jerked open his horn-handled old knife, and he

slashed off the legs of his tin breeches, his mackinaw pants and his overalls, just below his knees. He bit off a jaw-full of fire cut and then stood up, his fists on his hips, an unshaven cheek bulging with pepper-flavored tobacco, shapeless hat down over one eye, collar unbuttoned, suspenders stretching over his expanded chest, and—high mark of all high marks, distinction of distinctions—his pants ending in ragged edges below his knees. An inch of red drawers' legs showed below them, there followed bands of green wool socks, then black boot tops. Stagged pants! The finishing touch! Poetry was crushed to earth, never to rise triumphantly again in Paul Bunyan's camp. The inventive and prophetic Ford Fordsen had about killed it.

The great leader was delighted beyond words when he saw the loggers in their new costumes. He smiled indulgently when he heard some of the more modest among them saying that the brush would not bother them greatly now, and that Ford Fordsen's invention was a mighty good useful one. This is the reason loggers of to-day give for stagging their pants. But Paul Bunyan knew that his men had all taken up with the invention because it suited their natures, which had come back to them. Most of them indeed, admitted it. The loggers of our time should also be frank and admit that stagged pants spring from the he-bulliness of their souls. As Paul Bunyan said, "Etiquette, dainty speech, sweet scents, poetry and delicate clothes belong properly in the drawing-room, the study and the sanctum. They are hothouse growths. Loggers should take pride in hard labor and rough living. Anything that helps their Hesomeness makes them better men. All glory to you, Ford Fordsen, for the invention of stagged pants."

He offered the bunkhouse genius his little finger. Ford Fordsen got his arms a fourth of the way around it, and the two inventors shook hands.

The months went on and the loggers' rugged virtues continued to gain strength from the virile buffalo milk hot cakes. They did noble work among the sage trees and felled so many of them that the Big Swede and the blue ox had to go in a gallop during their working hours to snake all the logs to the landings.

Now, this was the year which is mentioned in history as the Year of the Hard Winter. But the bitterest cold could not now chill the blood of Paul Bunyan's He-Men. They had never been so jolly as they were this Christmas, and they jigged and chortled when Paul Bunyan gave each of them a knife devised especially for pants-stagging. The great leader had cut out thousands of these excellent presents from two of Babe's old ox shoes. This was the merriest holiday season the camp had ever known, and even the incredible cold of New Year's Day did not lessen the noisy bunkhouse gayety.

On the last night of the old year the mercury in the great thermometer which hung on the camp office had dropped to four hundred degrees below zero. Then the tube burst, and no one could tell the temperature, but it got appreciably colder. The next morning the boiling coffee froze on the stove, despite the desperate stoking of the kitchen firemen, and the loggers had to drink hot brown ice for their morning's breakfast. But they tramped cheerfully to work, nevertheless, cracking their mittened hands together and stamping the ground as they went along. They worked so hard to keep warm on this day that they talked and swore but little. This was fortunate. For on this incomparable New Year's Day every spoken word froze solidly in the air as soon as it was uttered. The next day the temperature rose, but the words remained frozen, and many a logger bumped his mouth by walking into the HELLOS and DAMNS which were solid in the air. But the hardy victims only laughed through their split lips at such accidents. These words all thawed out at once on a warmer day; they melted in one long-drawn-out, mournful echoing shout so unhumanly humorous in sound that the loggers rolled with laughter to hear it.

Cold as the winter was, Paul Bunyan and his men were reluctant to see it go, for every day had brought some tickling incident. But at last the gray frost crystals began to glitter occasionally from rays of sunshine which filtered through the white winter mists. Then Paul Bunyan began to plan for the hazardous historical drive down Moron River. Spring was at hand, and the great logger remembered his old whimsical query:

"If Springtime comes can Drives be far behind?"

The loggers, too, sensed the approach of the driving season, and every night the bunkhouses rang with sounds of filing, as the rivermen sharpened calks, pike

poles and peavies. They bellowed the old driving
songs as never before, and the floors shook as they
leaped and pranced to show the marvelous springi-
ness of their legs. They got so comradely in their
merriment and exuberance that the last poet among
them ventured a poem which began:

> "It's all very well to be profane,
>   When life is as dark as night;
>   But the man worth a fuss is the man who can cuss
>   When everything 'round him is bright."

He got no further, for in an instant one bully had
him down, chewing savagely on his ear, while others
raked his ribs with their calks. It was the last sigh
of poetry in the camp. Paul Bunyan heard about
it and had one of the happiest hours of his life as he
rejoiced over the good news.

"But every silver cloud has it shadows," he said
sensibly, when his exaltation had passed. "I still
expect great troubles and difficulties." He was wise
indeed in this thought, for he got a troublous problem
at once.

Sure as the great logger had been that the powerful buffalo milk hot cakes could only do good for his
loggers, sure as he was they could not give his men
too much red blood or make them too hellishly He,
Paul Bunyan had yet failed to reckon on the dire effects
that the virile food might have on weaker men. He
had given no thought to the scissor-bills who herded
and milked the buffalos. Throughout the fall these
men had shown nothing but their usual tameness and

amiability; during the Hard Winter they had shivered silently by their camp fires; but now they began to show that the powerful food was having a terrific effect on them. Many of the buffalos had died during the cold spell, and the scissor-bills had made pants from the shaggy hides. Some of the high-behinds had frozen also, and the scissor-bills had taken their skins and made tall, flapping hats of them. Colds had afflicted them during the winter, and for convenience they had tied their handkerchiefs around their necks. They took a fancy to this fashion and let the handker-chiefs remain after their colds were gone. Their next outbreak of virility was to unravel one of Babe's halter ropes and arrange a long little rope with a noose-end from each thread of it. They practiced throwing nooses over the posts of the buffalo corral fence until they became quite expert in casting them. The scissor-bills then caught wild horses with their ropes and broke them for riding. They got to be a crazy, noisy gang after this, and Paul Bunyan began to notice them as they rode through the sage trees, yipping shrilly. And then one morning they came to the hero-leader and requested that they be called "scissor-bills" no longer, but "buffalo boys" instead. Paul Bunyan admired their shaggy pants, their necker-chiefs and their tall hats, and he thoughtlessly consented to their wishes. He did not feel that the scissor-bills had it in them to become real He Men, but he was not a man to discourage worthy ambitions.

But Paul Bunyan soon had reason to remember one of his old sayings, that the road from the palace of generosity leads through a forest of perils. His one kindly gesture towards the lowly scissor-bills made them a powerful faction in the He Man country, and a fierce rivalry between them and the loggers soon developed. For they insisted on being called "buffalo boys," and Paul Bunyan's best men saw an intolerable dignity in the title. The buffalo boys painted large B. B's. on their hats, they painted the letters on the buffalos and on their horses also. At calving time they devised some irons in the shape of double B's., and they branded the buffalo calves with them. The buffalo boys grew even bolder; they began to ride among the bunkhouses in the evenings, yipping and yelling at the men who were earnestly preparing for the greatest drive of history.

Such impudence was not long tolerated, of course, and it got so that every morning found buffalo boys mourning for lost ears and doctoring the wounds made by sharp calks. But buffalo milk was running hot in their veins, and their new courage carried them to still greater extremes. One morning when the loggers came to work they found that every sage tree had B. B. burned into its bark. That day the drive was not talked about, for the loggers plotted vengeance as they toiled. This night they turned the buffalos out of the corral, and the buffalo boys were out until morning rounding up the herd. The following night they, in turn, galloped past the bunkhouses and roped every stovepipe that stuck above a roof. They dragged them into the timber and hid them, and the loggers had to dress by cold stoves the next morning.

That evening, during milking time, the loggers slipped into the buffalo boys' tents and poured water into their blankets; the next morning the loggers found their boots all filled with ice, for the buffalo boys had played such an evil trick on them during the night. The astonishing audacity of these lowly creatures was not to be longer endured.

Mark Beaucoup and his followers would not listen to the pleas of the moderates that the punishment of the buffalo boys be left until the drive was finished. The bunkhouse cranks had grown savage in the He Man country, and they now threw aside all restraint. They yelled their rage until all the loggers got excited; and in a short time the bunkhouses were empty, and the loggers were marching on the buffalo boys' camp. They closed in silently and attacked with lion-like ferocity. The buffalo boys, their timidity vanished now, stood up and gave vigorous battle. When Paul Bunyan stepped into camp and called, "Roll out, my bullies! Roll out for the big drive!" he got no answer. Then he looked toward the buffalo corral and saw a sea of dust surging over miles of the valley. All over the gray surface of this sea fists were flashing up as whitecaps jump and fall on wind-blown waters. Paul Bunyan leaped towards the scene of conflict.

But the great logger's endeavors to separate the fighters were vain. When he got among them he had to stand still for fear of trampling them; the buffalo boys and the loggers crowded against his feet as they clinched and punched, and some of them rolled under the arches of his boots. He ordered the factions to their camps, but they would not hear. Then Paul Bunyan bellowed. The battlers were all thrown down, but they bounced up fighting. Ears and fingers were now flying up everywhere in the dust, and the leader was alarmed by the thought that a more fearful condition was in sight than even poetry had threatened to bring about. The ferocious masculinity that his two gangs of men had got from the virile hot cakes would leave him with camps of earless and fingerless cripples. Disaster loomed over the logging industry once more.

His brain racing like a dynamo as it conceived desperate ideas, Paul Bunyan failed to notice at first that the dust sea had mysteriously vanished, though the struggle still raged. Not until he saw all the loggers and buffalo boys stop fighting and throw themselves on the ground, each man clutching at his own legs and howling with fear, did he realize that an unnatural happening was saving his men from exterminating each other. Every frantic fighter was howling, "My boots is runnin' over with blood! I'm a goner sure!"

Paul Bunyan heard them with amazement, and with amazement he gazed on the valleys and hills. A thin mist was rising from the ground. It vanished soon; then Paul Bunyan saw that rain was springing from the earth, falling up—if the term may be used—for many feet, and then dropping back again. The first shower had rained up the legs of the buffalo boys and the loggers, and they had mistaken it for blood. Now they were still rolling, moaning and bellowing. Paul

Bunyan's amazement soon passed, for he was accustomed to unnatural seasons, climates and happenings. He was all delight that the unusual rain had stopped the battle, and he saw no harm in it yet; he did not know that this was a rain of such tremendous force that it had poured through the earth. . . .

For this was the Spring That the Rain Came Up From China. . . .

Harder and harder the rain came up, and it was not long before the loggers and the buffalo boys opened their eyes and stopped their yelling. They were soaked all over now, and they knew that the sudden warm wetness of their legs had not been from blood. Paul Bunyan laughed through his beard, which was high and dry, when he saw his men begin to run for the camp to get out of the strange rain. The fight was forgotten, and the logging industry was saved.

The ground hissed as the rain came up with new violence. The drops became streams . . . the streams doubled. . . trebled . . . and in an hour there were ten streams where only one had come up before. The rain became a downpour—or an up-pour, rather. It got the proportions of a cloudburst—or, perhaps it should be said, an earthburst. The hillocks and hummocks had forests of small fountains. In the low places pools were forming, and these boiled with muddy foam as myriads of miniature geysers spurted up from them.

Paul Bunyan, feeling great satisfaction over the happy ending the rain had given to the conflict between his two tribes, did not at first realize the danger to his recent logging operations from the unnatural rain. When he did think of the logs piled along the river he ran swiftly to look after them. He was too late. Moron River had already risen far over its banks, and all of the brown, peeled sage logs, the fruit of a season's labor, were now tossing on a muddy flood. The rain was coming up through the river in sheets; torrents were pouring into the stream from every small gully. The water was rising at the rate of a foot a minute. It would soon be in the camp grounds. Paul Bunyan made no attempt to retrieve his lost logs; he now rushed to save his camp.

The loggers had turned their bunkhouses upside down, because the rain had come up through the floors. They had then set their bunks on the rafters, and they were now snug and dry, for the rain could not pour up through the tight roofs. The loggers left their cozy quarters reluctantly when they heard Paul Bunyan call, "Roll out or roll Up!" They could imagine nothing more disagreeable than its raining up their pants' legs, rough He Men though they were. But when they saw the river rising in rushing waves they did not need Paul Bunyan's orders to make them run for the cookhouse. Johnny Inkslinger was wiring the camp office and Babe's stable to the mammoth building, and the Big Swede was making his fastest moves since the Dakota days as he hitched up the blue ox. Paul Bunyan roared, "Yay, Babe!" just as the river waters thundered into camp. The blue ox plunged towards the Cascade Hills. He dragged the three greatest buildings of the camp and all the loggers to safety. But the bunkhouses were rolling over and over in the flood.

Paul Bunyan and his two aides saved two of the buffalo boys, two buffalos, two high-behinds, two tigermunks, two blond wolves, and two wild horses, from the raging waters, but all other life perished.

For forty days and forty nights it rained up from China, and then the flood receded. Paul Bunyan and his men looked down from the Cascades and saw that all of the old He Man country had been washed away. It was now a low valley. There was sage in it still, but this sage was only brush. Ridges and buttes of gray rock were all of the old land that remained. There was no longer any logging in the greater part of it. But here on the new slopes of the Cascades was a more cheering sight. For the old land over these slopes had covered a magnificent forest of white pine which was even finer than that around the old home camp. The loggers shouted when they saw it. And was it a tear, that gleam of moisture in Paul Bunyan's beard? If so, it was from his new happiness.

"It's an ill rain," he chuckled, "that brings no logger wood."

The two buffalo boys, like the loggers, still heroic from their virile winter's diet, had come through their ordeal in good shape and the buffalos had slept all the forty days and nights. But the other poor animals! The wild horses were wild no longer; they had become tame and would now eat sugar out of any man's hand. The buffalo boys nick-named them bronchos. The high-behinds, the blond wolves and the tigermunks were all cowards at heart, and they had been scared out of twenty years' growth. Not one of them was knee-high to a logger now. The Big Swede made his first and only joke about the tigermunks, who had been scared into the size of chips.

"Tigermunks!" he grinned. "Aye tank these har ban chipmunks!"

And chipmunks they have been called ever since. Paul Bunyan's history does not tell how the high-behinds came to be named jack rabbits, or how the blond wolves came to be named coyotes. No doubt they were also named humorously, for the loggers were gay when the rain no longer came up from China. Anyhow, the old names are no longer used in the He Man country.

EVIL INVENTIONS

PAUL BUNYAN knew nothing about women, but he had heard of them with little liking for the stories he heard. History, industry, invention and oratory were, to his mind, the four grand elements of human life. And women, as they were revealed in the loggers' stories, cared little about these elements. Women seemed to lack inventiveness especially, and this was man's greatest quality. Women, the great logger had heard, were often marvelous cooks; but men had invented both can-openers and doughnuts. Women were excellent makers of garments; but men had invented calked boots, mackinaws and stagged pants. Women were assiduous readers of poetry; but men had invented most of the poetry that these creatures cared about. Even in the writing of history, where inventiveness is not allowed (or *was* not, rather; for nowadays, such is progress, many historians are good inventors also), women had apparently done nothing. Paul Bunyan, in the early days of his camp, often marveled when he heard his loggers hurrahing and stamping as they talked about the people called pretty women. He himself could not see their use in the grand parts of life. But when he knew his men better he decided that women were creations of the loggers' fancies, that they were incredible and fabulous.

For Paul Bunyan's loggers only cared to feel effects; they had no wish to think about causes. They would make a reality out of any fancy that delighted them; they never inquired beyond their pleasures. When they were told that they were making history they heard the statement with a thrill, but they did not pretend to know what it was all about. As for inventions, they used them joyfully, but they thought that Paul Bunyan's new devices just happened. "We always sharpened our axes by rollin' rocks down-hill," the loggers would say. "We'd run alongside, holdin' the ax blades on the stones as they rolled. But in the Big Dust country they was no rocks an' no hills, so ol' Paul made grindstones." That was their story of the invention of the grindstone, an invention to which Paul Bunyan had given weeks of intense thought. And as for industry, why, a man just went out and did what old Paul told him to do. Oratory was great stuff; it made a man feel powerful good to listen to it; but, holy mackinaw! how was a man to remember all the things that old Paul said? But they did like oratory; yes, they liked it right well.

Now Paul Bunyan came to know that his men were great only in the performance of their work. They were not comprehenders and creators. They could hardly distinguish between knowledge and fancy. Thus the great logger came to doubt the existence of women. He came to consider all the loggers' ideas as fancies and drolleries, little men's nonsense. He seldom listened to them; and as time went on he forgot women along with the other notions with which the

loggers amused themselves.   In oration after oration
Paul Bunyan emphasized the fact that logging was the
greatest industry, and that loggers, therefore, were the
greatest laborers; they should have no pride or
thought outside the operations of Paul Bunyan.
They believed this finally; and then their bunkhouse
songs and stories were all about work in the woods
and the river drives, and women were very seldom
thought about.   Johnny Inkslinger's oratorical medicine swamped them with ideas one time; and later they
were seduced into poetry; but they had become bully
loggers again in the He Man country.

They would have kept the new innocency of their
souls, no doubt, had the forty-day flood been a week
shorter.   During the first week of the flood the loggers were excited about the strange rain which was
streaming up from China, then the muddy foaming
waters which filled the valley below their place of
refuge became a monotonous sight.   Some of them began to tease the buffalo boys, and others played with
the blond wolves, the high-behinds, the tigermunks
and the other animals which Paul Bunyan had brought
into the cookhouse.   But these wild creatures had been
so frightened by the flood that they would not learn
tricks.   Paul Bunyan invented picture cards for his
men and the games of poker, rummy and cribbage; but
the bunkhouse cranks were so violent at play that it
had to be given up.   Then the loggers could only tell
stories, and sing and jig for amusement.   During the
last week of the flood, camp stories being told out, the
loggers remembered women; and they became so in-

terested in songs and stories about them that they were
sorry when the flood was over and a spring day dawned
on a new green land. This morning Paul Bunyan
called, "Roll out or roll up!" but he got no answer.
The surprised leader stopped and looked into the cookhouse. He saw Shanty Boy and three other bards
standing with their arms over each other's shoulders.
The quartet was singing:

"Here I sit in jail, with my back to the wall;
    And a red-headed woman was the cause of it all!"

"Red-headed woman?" Paul Bunyan stroked his
beard in perplexity. "Woman? I think I have
heard that word before. Woman . . . m-m-m-hmm
. . . now I remember. Those creatures so strangely
fascinating to plain men. I doubted their existence.
At any rate, I hope we never meet with any. I have
had difficulties enough from ideas, poetry and floods.
My loggers shall now have hard work again and forget these tempting memories."

Once more he roared the noble call to labor. The
loggers heeded it this time, and they came out smiling blushingly. Thereupon Paul Bunyan made them
a straightforward speech, beguiling phrased, however;
and when it was done the loggers thought only of their
work tools and of the handsome, odorous timber which
covered the new slopes below them.

They got new tools from the camp office; and when
the sunlight made golden trails among the pine trees
the loggers were already wet with honest sweat, and

many trees had dropped from their cutting. They worked without great exertion, for they were soft from their long rest, and Paul Bunyan had warned them against sore muscles and exhaustion. As the sun rose higher the spring air got warm and drowsy, and it breathed a troublous languor into their beings. The loggers went to extremes in heeding Paul Bunyan's cautionary advice; and in the afternoon they toiled listlessly whenever they worked at all; but most of the time they leaned on their axes, or against trees, and expressed unusual wonderings. When the Big Swede remonstrated with them they replied that they felt weary and sore from their labor even now; old Paul would roar, they said, if they did not take care of their selves. They went on arguing loudly, neglecting their work, but the Big Swede had little time for argument. Babe, the blue ox, was now so exuberantly frisky in all his motions that the foreman had to watch him constantly. During this one short argument Babe had knocked down ten acres of trees with gay swings of his horns and had trampled them into splinters.

"Har noo!" yelled the Big Swede, hastily leaving the lazy loggers. And as Babe jerked him this way and that way, lashing the foreman with his lively tail and making playful pokes at him with his horns, the Big Swede grumbled, "By yeeminy! Aye tank dese crazy t'ings lak rain fall oop play hal with may yob!"

The Big Swede was easily discouraged, but Paul Bunyan had his usual hopefulness as he planned the reorganization of his camp. Johnny Inkslinger had left for the old home camp to discover how John

Shears and the great farm had fared in the flood and
to get Shagline Bill's endless freight team started with
loads of new supplies.   The great logger himself had
brought his workbench out of the camp office and set
it up at the edge of the new pine forest.   Then he
planned a sawmill.   It was not to be such a grand mill
as he had erected on Round River in the Leaning Pine
country; but he wanted a good one that would cut at
least 10,000,000 feet of lumber in twelve hours.   In
six months he should have enough lumber to make a
fair set of temporary bunkhouses for his men.   In the
meantime, it was good that the spring nights were so
cheerful and warm, as the loggers could sleep in the
open air without injury or even discomfort.

In a week the plans were finished, and, for a millhouse Paul Bunyan moved the back room of his camp
office over to the banks of the Moron River, which had
become a mature, decent, dependable stream since the
flood; and he put a big crew of his loggers to work,
making concrete beds for the saws and edgers and in-
stalling the mill machinery.   Work dropped to nearly
nothing in the woods.   Paul Bunyan left the mill construction under the supervision of Ford Fordsen, camp
tinker and the only bunkhouse inventor, and he went
into the woods to make his men get out logs for the
new mill.

Now Paul Bunyan was astonished and puzzled when
he heard his loggers re-telling the stories with which
they had amused themselves during the last week of
the flood.   Instead of working, one logger would lean

against a tree and remark that he had always liked a little flesh on them himself; and his partner would reply that every man had his own taste, but as for him, give him the cute little kind that a burly could tuck under one arm. Then a swamper would come up and say that he didn't care much about shape, but he did like red hair and a wide mouth. And a limber would join the group and say that he guessed he was peculiar, but he didn't have much use for the frolicksome ones, but he liked them quiet and sort of dreamy-eyed. Each man would argue at length for his own inclinations, carefully respecting, however, the preferences of the others.

Paul Bunyan lost patience upon hearing such nonsense; and he gave sharp orders that there was to be no more talking in the woods. Logs were needed for the new mill; his men were to get down to business and forget their vain imaginings; for it was doubtful if such fantastic creatures as they talked about really existed.

For the first time in camp history Paul Bunyan's loggers felt that their leader was driving them, and they worked sullenly. Their aroused memories troubled them greatly as the spring got more of languorous warmth, and it was torment for them to keep their thoughts to themselves as they worked. But at night they were free to speak; and as they lay in their blankets among the trees they talked for hours in soft voices, gazing dreamily at the moon and stars, and sighingly breathing the warm, odorous air of the

spring night.   And in their sleep, memories gave them
perilous dreams; and they rolled and tossed and pulled
covers and talked tenderly between snores.

But these memories—if they were *not* fancies—
were not so hurtful as poetry and ideas, for they
allowed the loggers to work, once Paul Bunyan had
stopped conversation about them.   When the new
mill was completed, the mill pond was black with logs.
Paul Bunyan came in from the woods, and Ford Fordsen showed him his finished work with pride.   The
boilers were loaded with steam, said the bunkhouse
genius; the rollers were in their oiled boxes, the chains
were over the sprockets, and the belts were tight
around the pulleys; and the great shining bandsaw
was waiting with sharp teeth for its first bite from a
pine log.

Paul Bunyan heard his fellow inventor with admiration, for there was no room for envy in the great
logger's soul.   He had an honest comradely smile
for Ford Fordsen as he lifted his hand and gave the
signal for the sawing to begin.   Now the exhausts
roared, the main shaft began to revolve, the chains
rattled and squeaked, and the rolls and pulleys
whirled.   But the great bandsaw did not move.   Ford
Fordsen ran into the mill to discover the trouble; he
returned at once, frowning a little, but not discon-
certed.

"A slight mistake, Mr. Bunyan," he said crisply.

"Yes?   Explain this slight mistake, Ford Fordsen."

"It is only a *slight* mistake.   But we will have to
rebuild the mill."

"Well; I am happy to hear that it is only a *slight* mistake," said Paul Bunyan. "You can rebuild the mill at once, I suppose."

"In six months perhaps. I prefer to make my own plans and invent some new machines that match my own ideas. I am rather glad of this *slight* mistake."

"Impudence!" roared Paul Bunyan. "Tell me at once what is wrong."

Ford Fordsen was thrown from his feet, but he got up with dignity.

"You have the advantage of me in size," he said pounding wrathfully with his fist on the great logger's toe. "But I, too, am an inventor now, and I claim equal rights with you in invention. You may have history, for history is bunk; you may have oratory, for your voice is larger than mine; and you may have industry, for you possess the blue ox. But as for invention——"

"Before you become an orator in spite of yourself tell me, as inventor to inventor, if you like, about this slight mistake," said Paul Bunyan calmly.

"But I have told you that the mill must be rebuilt!" said Ford Fordsen impatiently. "However, if you must know, the slight mistake is this: The men who put in the concrete base for the headrig got to talking about women, and their minds left their job. They ran concrete around the saw, and now the lower part of this hundred foot band is frozen as in solid rock. The mill, you see, must be rebuilt; and I must be about it."

"Women again!" grumbled Paul Bunyan. "If

they do not exist my men soon will have invented them. If they do exist in other lands it is easy to see why there is no great industry, no marvelous inventions and no making of history in any place but my camp. Even as memories or fancies they are nuisances. But here: I must attend to this cocky little fellow."

He reached down and seized Ford Fordsen between his thumb and forefinger and then raised him to a level with his eyes.

"Your grand and exceptional notions trouble my poor head," said Paul Bunyan, "so I must work with my own simple ideas. You shall be at work with your felling ax once more this afternoon."

"I warn you that I'll not do foul, sweaty labor again, Mr. Bunyan," said Ford Fordsen composedly. "If you put me back in the woods I'll preach the ten-hour day to the loggers. And I ask you to return me to the ground. I find this high altitude uncomfortable."

"Audacity!" exclaimed Paul Bunyan, so astonished that he nearly dropped this astonishing bunkhouse genius. "The ten-hour day! Thunderation! What an unheard of thing! Is the sun shining? Do I wear whiskers? Do men chew with their teeth? Is Babe a blue ox? And—do loggers work twelve hours a day? What devils do trail me! Ideas; poetry; floods; women; the ten-hour day—what next? By the holy old, roaring old, oily old——"

What would certainly have been the grandest curse of history was interrupted by the appearance of Johnny Inkslinger on the summits of the Cascades.

Paul Bunyan's wrath and chagrin vanished and the light shone once more into his eyes as his interested gaze followed the timekeeper's progress. Shagline Bill's endless freight team circled down the mountains behind Johnny Inkslinger. Paul Bunyan dropped Ford Fordsen carelessly into his pocket and stepped up the slopes to hear the news.

Johnny Inkslinger had a condensed report of fifteen thousand, seven hundred and twenty-one pages which dealt with the destruction of the great farm and the transformation of the Smiling River country in the unnatural rain. But he gave a more cheerful account of a new country which he had discovered. It was just over the mountains, he said, in the region called Nowaday Valley. There he had procured a good load of camp supplies. There were people in that country, the timekeeper went on to say, people of a very strange sort. He described them, and he ended his description by doubting if even one out of a hundred of these people could become a logger. Some were too ponderous, others were marvelously fragile, and everyone held an ax awkwardly.

"I have heard of such creatures," said Paul Bunyan. "They are real, then. But not another word must be spoken about them. If my loggers were to hear that some of this species which they remember so ardently were at hand, I'd have more trouble than poetry gave me. We must keep this a secret, Johnny Inkslinger."

Then they rose and walked over to the cookhouse, where the kitchen crew was unloading the freight

wagons. Paul Bunyan had forgotten Ford Fordsen.
But the impertinent bunkhouse genius had escaped
from the pocket during the conversation. He now
journeyed towards the woods, where the loggers were
doing little but talk over their memories. And it is not
difficult to imagine how much work was done after
the enraged inventor arrived with his news of Johnny
Inkslinger's discovery.

Paul Bunyan, with energy that was unusual even
for him, at once began to put the mill in a condition
to operate. It was a good mill as it stood, outside
of the solid saw, and he did not intend to rebuild it.
That would take time, and he wanted to have new
bunkhouses and the old camp routine as soon as possible. In order to keep his men from thinking about
their troublesome memories it was necessary to have
most of them in the woods again and to be with them
himself. Then the bunkhouse bards would start the
camp stories and songs once more, and the loggers
would be protected at night also. So, to work.

Experienced as he was with inventing, Paul Bunyan
was not long in getting an idea which solved his
problem. First, he had the loggers who were detailed
on mill construction build blocks of concrete under the
floor beams of the millhouse. While they were com-
pleting this labor he got one of his old inventions and
made many new models of it. This invention was
the steam-drive potato masher, which he had devised
for Hot Biscuit Slim, after the chief cook had originated mashed potatoes. In this invention Paul Bunyan had made the first known use of the steam cylinder.

He now took a battery of steam-drive potato mashers and installed them on the new concrete blocks under the mill.   Steam pipes were connected between them; and the new mill system was ready for a trial.

Paul Bunyan wiped the sweat from his dripping eyebrows and wrung out his beard; then he gave the signal to turn on steam.   The potato mashers pumped up and down perfectly at the rate of five hundred strokes a minute.   Each stroke thrust the mill building up forty feet and down forty feet.   The big carriage moved forward, carrying a pine log; the solid saw met its bark and grain; then the log carriage, flashing up and down with the millhouse, moved swiftly ahead, and the first cant dropped on the rolls.   The new mill was a success!   Paul Bunyan's inventive mind had triumphed again!   True, the mill men got a little seasick from going forty feet up and forty feet down five hundred times a minute; but they soon got accustomed to this and declared that they preferred the bouncing saw mill to the ordinary quiet kind.

Now Paul Bunyan remembered Ford Fordsen.

"You would rebuild a mill because of a slight mistake," he chuckled, reaching into his pocket for the bunkhouse genius.   "Come now; I will show you how really simple it was to solve the problem of the solid saw."

But Ford Fordsen was not in Paul Bunyan's pocket, of course.   He had not been there for a long time. Paul Bunyan quickly guessed that the bunkhouse genius had escaped while his leader was seated.   The great logger's last sitting had happened just one month ago, when he heard his returning timekeeper's report.

Certainly Ford Fordsen had gone to the woods with news of Johnny Inkslinger's discovery.

Knowing the difficulties which the Big Swede had been having with the blue ox, knowing also the foreman's lack of oratorical powers, Paul Bunyan feared greatly for his loggers. He ran at once for the timber where they were supposed to be working. The loggers were gone, and their felling tools also. And neither the Big Swede nor the blue ox was anywhere in the woods. The boughs of the last felled trees were already dead and dry and the stumps of these trees were browned by the suns of many days. The woods were still but for the wind whispers, and the breathing silence of the deserted timberland was mournful to the great logger. His was a somber, frowning countenance as he returned to camp. He looked in Babe's empty stable before he passed, and two dark objects in the manger attracted him curiously. They were strange engines, and not of his devising. He had not seen their like before. He could lift one in his two hands; and he did so, turning it around and around, observing its upright boiler, its drums and cables, and the hewn logs to which it was bolted. Wondering how the engines had come to the manger, Paul Bunyan put them in his two mackinaw pockets and tramped on over the mountain towards Nowaday Valley, knowing that there he would find his loggers.

It was late afternoon when the leader-hero reached the Big Fir timber which covered the slopes around Nowaday Valley. Through the trees he saw a blue that was bluer than the sky. Babe mooed gently as his master approached, but his gaze remained fixed on the border where the green valley floor met the timber. Smoke was rising there; and now Paul Bunyan saw roofs and people among the firs.

"My loggers and the women folks," said Paul Bunyan, not very cheerfully.

He strode on through the forest, and ere long he saw that smoke was coming from such an engine as he had in his pockets. Ford Fordsen was at the levers; now he jerked one, and a drum revolved swiftly, winding a cable which whipped and slashed underbrush as it was hauled from the timber. Then a big log to which the cable was fastened crashed through the small trees, plowing a deep furrow as it was dragged on. Now Ford Fordsen jerked another lever, the big log was lifted, and then it was lowered easily to a car which was standing on two shining steel rails. . . .

A whistle shrilled. Paul Bunyan saw his loggers coming in droves from the woods. Ford Fordsen left his engine and approached the great logger.

"So the inventor has become the industrialist also," said Paul Bunyan grimly. "I suppose you will now compete with me in oratory——"

"That is my affair." Ford Fordsen interrupted his old leader coolly. "My only business with you, Mr. Bunyan, is to inform you that you must keep your ox away from my donkeys."

"Donkeys?"

"I have named my skidding machines donkey engines. Your ox, your skidding machine, made cunning and conscienceless from jealousy, has escaped from your foreman; he waits until night; then he plunges out of the woods, seizes my engine in his teeth and makes away with it. He has stolen two of them. I demand their return."

Paul Bunyan drew them from his pocket and dropped them to the ground.

"I do not care about your donkeys, your engines, your skidding machines," said the great logger. "I have come for my men."

"Try and get them," said Ford Fordsen amiably.

"You may have learned inventing and industry," said Paul Bunyan. "And you despise history. But I shall now teach you the worth of oratory."

"I grant you the privilege of attempting it," said Ford Fordsen pleasantly. "Instead of giving the loggers oratory I have given them the ten-hour day. And they have found other things."

Paul Bunyan would not argue the merits of the ten-hour day with Ford Fordsen. Regretting that he had ever encouraged this man by praising his one noble invention, stagged pants, the great logger said no more, but went on into Nowaday Valley. He stopped at a place where there were many cottages. They were evidently used for bunkhouses by his loggers, as the men had come this way after leaving the woods. They were curious bunkhouses indeed, for the walls of each one were painted in bright colors; there were curtains in the windows, and every bunkhouse had a neat and pretty yard of grass and flowers. Paul Bunyan thought it strange that his bully loggers should tolerate this; but he did not allow the thought to trouble him. He began to speak with his rarest eloquence.

If he had delivered such an oration in the old home camp his men would have listened to him for days without thinking of eating or sleep. They would have been moved continuously by whatever emotions the sounds of the orator's rich phrases evoked; and at the end they would have obeyed his most extravagant wish.

But now the loggers did not even come out of their bright bunkhouses to hear him. Now and again a face appeared at a window or in a doorway, but it was always the face of one of the women folk, seeming hostile or curious, but otherwise unmoved. Knowing that his oratorical powers had never been greater, Paul Bunyan was at last affected by a fear that the loggers were now ruled by a force stronger than his own. He put even more vigor and color into his oration, but he now spoke with less confidence. . . .

Then one of the women folk came out of the bunkhouse. She stopped and looked up at the great logger with brave curiosity; and he in turn was so perplexed by the strange sight of this creature, who had something of the appearance of a logger, but was yet so unlike one, that he studied her and abandoned his oration. Was it possible that such frail and useless-seeming creatures could have powers surpassing his own?

Then Paul Bunyan did what every true man, whether ditch-digger or king, has often longed painfully to do. He now did that which men are forever attempting in their imaginings. He lifted the woman person in his hand and observed her as a naturalist observes a small kitten or a mouse.

This specimen of the women folk did not seem to mind the liberty which Paul Bunyan took with her. She sat comfortably in his hand, with her ankles crossed, and opened a case which hung from her arm; she gazed unconcernedly into a mirror which was in the lid of this case; then she patted powder on her nose and cheeks, turning her head first this way and then that way.

Paul Bunyan could not understand this woman person. She could not be explained by any of his ideas. She looked even less like a logger, now that he saw her closely. Her feet, for one thing, were ridiculously small, and the thin-soled slippers on them would not last a day at work in the woods. Her socks were of transparent, shimmering stuff, and they were pink, like the New Iowa clover. He had never seen anything except a cook's apron which was like the garment she wore, and he had never seen anything at all compared with the curving soft shapes revealed in this garment. Her face was something like a boy logger's face, but her eyes were not boy's eyes; for some different spirit shone in their brown lights. Her strangely cut hair was combed straight down over her forehead and its clipped ends made an even line above eyebrows which were no greater than threads. Her arms were round and white and firmly fleshed, but they seemed to have little muscle. Her small hands surely could not reach around an ax handle; nevertheless she was proud of them, for she now polished her fingernails on her pink socks and then admired the new glitter of them.

"I still do not understand this woman person," whispered Paul Bunyan to himself. "I have observed her closely, but the secret of her power is not yet known to me. Surely my bully loggers will yet prefer my oratory to these weak women folk. I must try again."

The woman person looked up at the gusty murmur; and on her small red mouth, and in her sunny brown eyes, was a smile. And Paul Bunyan saw also the tiniest of cups in each of her powdered cheeks. These, too, were marvelous and new to him.

"I have had an adventure which I can talk about for a long time," said the woman person. "Now put me down."

Paul Bunyan marveled still more at the imperiousness of this voice, which was yet so soft, so gentle and low. He had seen one logger chew off another's ear for less arrogant words. And now that he looked for them he did not discover ears on this woman person. But she had certainly not profited by the lesson.

"You have not yet learned bunkhouse courtesy?" asked Paul Bunyan conversationally.

The woman person shrugged her shoulders and wrinkled her nose. She seemed to consider this a good enough answer, for she did not speak. Paul Bunyan wanted to chide her, and he was surprised that he found no words for it. He felt embarrassment.

"Tell me, please," he said bashfully, "how you women folk won my loggers."

"Oh!" she replied, blushing a little, "we wanted husbands and babies."

More mysteries! More words without meaning to

him! This was an explanation perhaps, but it explained nothing.

Now the woman person grasped two hairs of Paul Bunyan's beard, one in each small hand, and pulled them playfully, smiling such a smile as he had never seen on any logger's face.

"You must go away, you know," she said softly. "We are all so happy here."

Paul Bunyan heard a pleading strain in her strange singing voice, but he could not interpret this sound. He saw her wistfully smiling eyes and mouth, but he could not read what he saw on her face. He felt the softness of the woman person in his hand—and he understood her a little. He learned something of her strength, alien as it was to any strength he had known. And he thought: I have lost my loggers; for neither history, invention, industry nor oratory can prevail with them against this woman person.

Gently Paul Bunyan put her on the ground. The woman person's walk was like a dance as she left him. In the door of her bright bunkhouse she turned and blew him a kiss. And was gone. Paul Bunyan waved his hand. The gesture was not for the woman person; it was a farewell to his loggers.

Paul Bunyan spoke no more; but he returned to his camp at once, taking the blue ox with him over the mountains. He told his remaining men of the women folk and let them go. Soon or late he would lose them, and he let them go now, that they might not be held too long from their desire. . . .

The sinking sun flashed its last blaze of red over a

camp that was deserted of all save the great heroes and the mighty blue ox. The Big Swede had returned and he slept; Johnny Inkslinger figured; and Babe mooed dolorously as the shadows clouded the silent timber. And Paul Bunyan, the supreme inventor, the noble historian, the master orator, the grand field marshal of industry, mused in sad resignation on the vanity of man's enterprises. The logging industry, which he had invented, would go on as long as trees grew from the earth, and his name would be heard forever on the tongues of men. He would have power, but it would be only the power of a vast spirit breathing in the dark, deep woods. He would have the glory he had dreamed about in his beginnings . . . but glory was a poor consolation . . . his life work was done. . . .

The shadows got dense . . . the shapes of the heroes, and the shape of Babe, the blue ox, and the shapes of buildings, mountains and trees merged in the darkness. And there history leaves them.

COMSTOCK EDITIONS
A bookshelf filled with the
rich tradition of the American West

Tough Trip Through Paradise, Andrew Garcia.
An unforgettable portrait of the last days of the
frontier from the recently discovered diaries of
a man who lived among the Indians.

008-2 $3.95

Trask, Don Berry. A novel of the first encoun-
ters of the mountain men and the Indians of
the Northwest coast. A classic.   001-5 $3.95

A Majority of Scoundrels, Don Berry. The au-
thentic story of the legendary trader-trappers of
the Rocky Mountain Fur Country and the opening of the Mountain West.   028-7 $3.95

The Big Four, Oscar Lewis. The story of the
building of the Central Pacific Railroad and the
men behind it—Stanford, Hopkins, Crocker, and
Huntington.   042-2 $4.50

The Flying North, Jean Potter. The story of
the bush pilots of Alaska based on interviews
and first-hand accounts. An amazing story of
pioneering aviation.   018-X $3.95

We hope you can find these books at your local
bookstore. If not, you can order them from us
by sending a check or money order for the price
of the book plus one dollar for the first copy
and seventy-five cents for each additional copy.
A free catalog of Comstock books is available
from this address:

Comstock Editions, Inc., Dept. 457
3030 Bridgeway Blvd.
Sausalito, CA 94965